STRUCTURED
CHAOS

STRUCTURED
CHAOS

THE UNUSUAL LIFE OF A CLIMBER

VICTOR SAUNDERS

Vertebrate Publishing, Sheffield
www.v-publishing.co.uk

STRUCTURED
CHAOS
VICTOR SAUNDERS

First published in 2021 by Vertebrate Publishing. This paperback edition first published in 2022.

 Vertebrate Publishing
Omega Court, 352 Cemetery Road, Sheffield S11 8FT, United Kingdom.
www.v-publishing.co.uk

Front cover: On Spantik in 1987, where Victor Saunders and Mick Fowler
(pictured) made the first ascent of the Golden Pillar. © Victor Saunders.
Photography copyright © Victor Saunders unless otherwise credited.

This book is a work of non-fiction. The author has stated to the publishers that, except in such minor respects not affecting
the substantial accuracy of the work, the contents of the book are true.

A CIP catalogue record for this book is available from the British Library.

ISBN: 978-1-912560-67-7 (Paperback)
ISBN: 978-1-912560-68-4 (Ebook)
ISBN: 978-1-912560-69-1 (Audiobook)

10 9 8 7 6 5 4 3 2 1

Cover design by Rosie Edwards, Vertebrate Publishing.
Production by Cameron Bonser, Vertebrate Publishing.
www.v-publishing.co.uk

Vertebrate Publishing is committed to printing on paper from sustainable sources.

Printed and bound in the UK by TJ Books Limited, Padstow, Cornwall.

CONTENTS

FOREWORD

BY MICK FOWLER

Victor Saunders is a remarkable man. Over his seventy years he must have accumulated the potential for a near-unlimited number of riveting real-life short stories. 'Structured chaos' is the way he describes his life so far – but it has been a wonderfully productive kind of chaos. Whether it be on extreme mountain adventures or in social situations, Victor's writing brings out that he invariably leaves a deep impression on those that meet him. After our first meeting, in Chamonix high street, I was so bowled over by his irrepressible questioning about a route I had just climbed that I cheekily wrote that I found him an 'irritating little squirt'. He responded by writing that he found me 'insufferably arrogant'. And so started a deep friendship that has endured for over forty years. That ever-questioning side of his personality is still there, of course – and it resonates strongly throughout this book. He moves in an ever-inquisitive manner from one adventure to the next; the reader will soon appreciate that he is a man of many talents and a master at self-deprecation. That chaos he refers to should not mask the intelligence and focus that has led to award-winning books, six ascents of Everest, the longest sea-cliff traverse in Britain, and a host of adventurous first ascents on rock, on ice and in the Himalaya.

But this book is not so much about achievements. It is about friendships, personalities, experiences and a journey through life. Whether it be harsh bullying at school, sweatshop labour in ships, saving lives, traversing mud cliffs or pushing boundaries in the Himalaya, his sharp prose weaves the different facets of his varied life into a vivid and immensely enjoyable read. Read on and be prepared to be left reeling at the breadth and number of intense experiences that he has squeezed in so far. And he is still going strong.

Mick Fowler
September 2020

PRELUDE

Mountains have given structure to my adult life. I suppose they have also given me purpose, though I still can't guess what that purpose might be. And although I have glimpsed the view from the mountaintop and I still have some memory of what direction life is meant to be going in, I usually lose sight of the wood for the trees. In other words, I, like most of us, have lived a life of structured chaos.

A mountaineer's life is not without risk. Although that's rather obvious, isn't it? And anyway, all lives contain risk. As for managing those risks, we like to think that's all about making good decisions, in day-to-day life as well as in the mountains. Even though good decisions are based on experience, which in turn is gathered from the consequences of bad ones. Well, perhaps. We tell ourselves, this way lies truth and that way lies … well, just that: lies. We try to look ahead, to envision the destination, as we stagger, sometimes knowingly, more often blindly, through the dark forest of decision trees that make up our existence.

On this confusing journey, this wandering through the woods, my best guides have been my unspeakable friends with their incomprehensible ideas and impossible beliefs. Decisions are made difficult because I believe, like most of my friends, in many contradictory things.

Here's an example: the Sybarite's Creed and the Climber's Creed.

Sybarite's Creed: Never bivouac if you can camp. Never camp if there is a hut. Never sleep in a hut if you can book a hotel.

Climber's Creed: If you were not cold, you had too many clothes. If you were not hungry, you carried too much food. If you were not frightened, you had too much equipment. If you got up the climb, well, it was too easy.

I believe in both creeds, wholeheartedly and without reservation.

I got to be this way not through design or planning, but through Brownian motion, following an erratic path, knocked this way and that by people, mostly those self-same unspeakable friends.

It has taken me a lifetime to realise that, all the while, it was people and not places I valued most. I have now been on more than ninety expeditions, accumulating seven years under canvas. I have climbed on all continents, many of the trips involving big adventures and occasional first ascents. And yet it is not the mountains that remain with me but the friendships. In 1940 Colin Kirkus said: 'going to the right place, at the right time, with the right people is all that really matters. What one does is purely incidental.'

This book is about what really matters.

1

PEKAN

(1954–1961)

Each time I'd woken during the journey, as the night bus from Singapore lurched from one pothole to the next, I'd seen a strange, obsessed look on the driver's face. Sometimes he would gun the engine until the bus was taking corners on two wheels. I managed several times to get back to sleep, but dreamt only of news headlines:

BUS PLUNGE IN PAHANG!
Sixteen killed, including lone foreigner! The Kuantan News Agency reports that bodies were difficult to identify after the high-speed crash, probably the result of driver error. The Kuantan News Agency ...

'Kuantan! Wake UP! This Kuantan. KUANTAN!'
  I rubbed my eyes and staggered off the bus. The driver really had been in a hurry; it was 4.30 a.m. and we weren't due in for another two hours. Yet here we were: safe, alive and early in Kuantan, the main city on the east coast of Peninsular Malaysia. My next bus, to the small town of Pekan, left in an hour. At the station cafe, a group of road people, Malaysians and Thais and Cambodians, were having an early morning breakfast. I joined them. *Roti chenai* and tea made with condensed milk. The *roti* was a particularly skilful effort, the cook spinning out the dough into crêpe-thin pancakes before folding them

1

over into small buns, and serving them with coconut curry sauce. But I was still half asleep when the local bus arrived, the slow coach to Pekan, slow because it stopped every few minutes for school-children and agricultural workers along the way. I began to think that reaching Pekan was analogous to a mountain climb, not least for the persistence in goal-seeking.

I had come here in the year 2000 looking for a connection with my childhood. Pekan is where I spent the first decade of my life, running around half naked in the tropical rain and sun with my younger brother, Christopher. We did not know it then, but in hindsight it was paradise. After growing up in the Elysian jungles of Malaysia, we returned to the British Isles, where Christopher and I were incarcerated in a miserable Scottish boarding school.

By then our parents had separated completely. Our father, George, ran a small import business in Gloucester. Our mother, Raiza, scraped together a pauper's living in London. I remember how she had once visited us at school, taking the train to Aberdeen, missing the connection and, in order not to give up spending a few hours with us, taking a taxi to the school. This was in 1963, when a cab ride of that length was more than a week's wages for most people; it must have taken my mother months to save for the journey. But her visit was the best gift of my childhood. This obsession with seeing journeys through, I inherited from her.

I had arrived in Singapore fresh from the Himalaya, although 'fresh' isn't perhaps the right word. You don't arrive anywhere fresh from a Himalayan climb. I had arrived worn out from a spell of exploration and the first ascent of Khoz Sar, a 6,000-metre mountain near the Pakistan–China border, climbing with Phil Bowker, a software engineer from Belfast. In Singapore, I had been the guest of the Singapore Mountaineering Association, which like its hometown was in the ascendance. In the 1990s its members had organised a series of bold expeditions with near-Teutonic planning, culminating in an ascent of Everest. My lecture was done, and now I had three days spare.

Three days in which to rediscover my childhood home on the edge of the Malayan jungle. After that I would go home.

'Pekan! Wake up! Pekan!' Damn. Sleeping once more, I had missed the procession of *kampongs* (villages) and jungle clearings, the new bridge and the fast new road from Kuantan to the royal town of Pekan. When I was last here there was at least one river to ford and, just before Pekan, a long wire-drawn car ferry. The journey used to take all day. It was now only late morning and the tropical sun was still taking hold. I stepped out into it, hardly able to believe what I was seeing. After forty years, I was back in my childhood home.

My old guidebook described Pekan as a sleepy town: that much was still correct. The rest of the book was horribly out of date. It had mixed up the mosques and the guesthouses; it said there was nothing to detain the visitor and that the food was uninspiring. The book was wrong on each of those counts, though to enjoy food it does help if you're prepared to eat what the locals do. The ancient Malays called themselves *Orang Laut*, 'the Sea People', and of course Pekan is a coastal village, so the traditional sustenance is fish and rice. If you eat fish and rice, you will eat well here.

The Pekan Guest House was incorrectly identified in the guidebook as the Government Rest House; it had not been called that for some time. The book was also out of date in recommending it as the best place to stay in town. Most of the buildings on the estuary front were rickety timber-frame shops with shuttered windows, their fading paint once green and blue. The houses seemed to be leaning sideways against each other. It was a timeless terrace, straight out of illustrations from the 1800s, a scene Joseph Conrad would have recognised. The guesthouse buttressed the end of the terrace but came from a different era, built with earthquake-resistant concrete columns and beams, the painted panels peeling and the entrance door slightly askew and open. This building looked even more unkempt than the timeless terrace.

I spent an hour in the threadbare sitting room, banging about a bit on the concierge's rickety desk, ringing the hand bell, then wandering round the deserted kitchen, where last night's dishes were still waiting to be washed up. Eventually, I heard a giggle and a girl's sleepy-eyed face peeped round the door. Another young woman soon joined her, both of them dressed in loose silk pyjamas. They didn't speak English and I couldn't manage more than 'Tidak cakap Malayu.' Later, I don't know how much later, another guest appeared, a man in T-shirt and sarong who, to judge by the sounds behind him, was with his children and wife.

'You can' check ou' too?'

'No, I can't check in!'

'Oh. Sin' las' nigh' is bin li'e this. I wan' check ou' too. But no one to atten' to us!'

I gave up at this point and went back into the sun. A one-street town with *kampong* architecture it might be, but Pekan boasts no less than three cybercafes. Two were filled with kids screaming as they played video games. The third was quieter, and run by a pair of shawl-headed girls who said the Chief's Rest House was quite good. I decided to try it, in spite of the guide's hostile review.

The guesthouse lay at the northern end of town, where a pair of giant concrete elephant tusks marked the entrance to the royal quarter, the palace and the polo grounds. Huge acacias and towering *kampong* mango trees lined the road, offering shade. The Chief's was a beautifully restored colonial stilt-house, with clean rooms and high ceilings. At ten dollars a night, it was expensive by Malaysian village standards, but very clean, with newly varnished wooden floors and rattan furniture. Outside, tropical fruit trees decorated the garden. There were bananas, of course, but also lengkuas, tapioca and guava. I took a shower and wandered back to town.

My reintroduction to Pekan food was at Mohammed Latif's restaurant, set back from the main street, and run by Musul, a sixty-four-year-old chef who had lived in Pekan all his life. He would have lived here when I grew up. I asked if he remembered a small white house on stilts, near a football field. He said there had only ever been one football field, the one by the Pekan Guest House.

Musul made very sweet tea with condensed milk and put on the table before me a banana leaf plate loaded with *nasi puteh* and *ikan kampong*. Here at last were the flavours of my childhood. The visual memories of Pekan might need to be rationalised, but the smells and tastes evoked my earliest memories without the need for any further interpretation. As I soaked up the aromas of my first years, I began to feel them less as memories and more as the overwhelming emotions of a relived childhood. These are the memories that get laid down before you have a name for them, the memories that prove there is no inevitable link between name and concept; with these memories, you know that this taste fully recalls that emotion. There is no name for it; you just know. My taste buds had taken me directly to a place my intellect could never reach.

The tropical air was heavy with the threat of rain as I went to look for our old house. Following Musul's advice, I headed to the football pitch first. At the far end of the ground, roughly where I remembered looking out at the football, were the stilts of what must have been a substantial house.

The house was gone. Timber houses don't last very long here; termites and the jungle see to that. The site had become overrun with ground vines and morning glory, tapioca and guava and plants that I could not recognise. It was a bit like stumbling on one of those lost jungle temples. There were some huge old mango trees at the back of what must have once been a garden. I couldn't be certain, but it seemed likely this was all that was left of our family home. I'd been halfway across the world to find our old house. And now, after thirty seconds, the quest seemed over. Perhaps it was like so many things in life: you dream and struggle for the goal, and when you reach it, the moment turns out to be ephemeral.

I took two snapshots and wondered what to do next. The sky was growing black, and the air ever more humid. Across the pitch was a vaguely municipal-looking building, which on closer inspection proved to be the town council offices. With perfect timing, it began to rain warmly as I walked in. Here I met the most helpful bureaucrats I had met in years, though possibly this was because I provided some kind of diversion. I don't suppose Pekan's local authority is often troubled by lost foreigners.

When I explained my quest and asked if they had any old plans or documents, they said there was one house that might have been ours; it had been called the Magistrate's House, the same one whose remains I'd just seen. The archives had some old plans and a photograph. Looking at the plans, it all came back: there was my bedroom, and there was the dining room, connected by a walkway to the kitchen. Here were the stilts our house sat on that allowed chickens to shelter from the sun and rain under the floor. This had been our house. It was gone, overgrown, but still remembered. Now I could go. *Nunc Dimittis.*

The rain had stopped and the sky was clearing; the sun returned and was soon busy driving away the last wispy clouds. I splashed across the football pitch, remembering that in the monsoon people used to cross it by boat, and in the dry season there were sometimes shadow puppet plays on white sheets hung between the goalposts.

There was one more place I wanted to revisit. A little south of Pekan is the vast beach of Enam Belas. The name means 'sixteen', indicating the mile marker from Pekan, or perhaps the extent of the sands. It must be one of the most isolated stretches of palm-fringed silver sands anywhere: miles and miles of curving beach, and no one else in sight. There used to be turtles here. According to one guidebook, there were 10,155 marine turtles on the east coast north of Kuantan in 1956, but by 1997 just twenty-seven were left. Pekan is south of Kuantan, but presumably the marine turtle figures for this coastline will be similar.

A gentle surf was rolling in from the impeccably regular lines of waves. The water was warm, but cooler than the sun, so, stripping off my T-shirt, I ran into the South China Sea, diving through the wave crests. I spent the next hour bodysurfing before I began having doubts. There used to be a strong tidal rip here, I recalled. And then

I asked myself, what if a shoal of jellyfish or a hungry shark turned up? I was quite alone and began imagining headlines again:

LONE SWIMMER DISAPPEARS!
Kuantan News Agency reports body of foreign swimmer
found nibbled by fish, missing body parts.

Suddenly I found myself pounding the water hard on my way back to shore.

I had asked the taxi driver to pick me up in two hours, so I spent my second hour under a coconut palm and read a bit. It was a strangely lonely experience on that desolate beach with only memories of water fights with my brother for company. Also, I realised I just don't feel as confident in the ocean as I do on mountains. When avalanches or crevasses threaten, I feel comfortable with my assessment of the risk. Not at the ocean. And there was one other thing: without the protection of my T-shirt, my back had turned red. Soon it was going to feel as if it had been flayed. But I didn't mind any of this; I was at Enam Belas again.

In the Chief's Rest House, my room had an air conditioner as well as a fan, but Pekan didn't seem to be oppressively hot, and a quick tepid shower soon did wonders for my blood temperature. The fan chopped the air above the bed; I lay stretched out on the freshly pressed cotton sheets and soon fell asleep to dream of water fights, cascading monsoon rains, paddling village boats across the football pitch, lightning and rolling thunder.

Thunder? No, that wasn't thunder; the noise was a knocking on the door. The door opened slightly to reveal a round face with a big gap-toothed smile. He said he was called Hamidi and had been out of his office when I visited the municipal building earlier that day.

'I want to hear your story too.'

I explained about the football pitch, the remains of the Magistrate's House, and the beach at Enam Belas. 'Come with me,' Hamidi said and pointed at his motorbike. Then he took me on a bumpy tour of the town. He showed me the school, the old timber classrooms replaced with concrete blocks. Hamidi was eight years younger than me, so we must have had the same teachers. The main thing I remember about that school was playing truant.

Hamidi then showed me the hospital, the two mosques, the several ancient palaces (one was now a museum, another a library) and so on. Pekan is the traditional home to the sultans of Pahang, each incumbent apparently erecting his own palace rather than moving into a second-hand home. Then there was the Royal Pahang Polo Club. I had to have a photograph of that; and then, teetering on the back of Hamidi's machine, we went down to the stables. One of the older grooms asked my father's name. Ah, yes, he remembered something about that. And there was also Li Saunders; did we know him? No? The groom directed us to a small *kampong* on the southern outskirts of the town. Pekan is slowly absorbing these outlying villages into its suburbs. Li Saunders? That was a coincidence. Hamidi thought it would be a good idea to find him. After all, how many people called Saunders can there have been in Pekan?

The house we were looking for was overhung by tall jungly trees and had been built like most of the *kampong* houses here: timber frame, shiplapped panels and high wooden stilts to protect them from monsoon floods. Chickens were clucking and scraping under the house as Hamidi's spluttering motorbike bumped to a halt by the wooden steps.

Inside, there were cool airy rooms, ageing rattan furniture and frames with fading family photographs. A sixty-year-old woman, Aziza, the widow of Razali, welcomed us and yes, she knew the Saunders family, because Razali had been my father's driver, and the only grown-up who used to play with us.

A big man, Razali would twirl us with his arms, and throw us in the air. We were inordinately fond of him and called him Rosy-Lee. Aziza asked which of the two children I had been; she used our nicknames, Anki and Kiki, and then smiled widely. She said that here, in this very house, we used to play, and often stayed the night. I was in the house of our *ama*, our Malaysian nanny. Aziza introduced me to two of her own children and a grandchild. Then she showed me a nostalgic set of photographs. There was the strong young Razali and Aziza seated with their first child. Next, in exactly the same pose, with the same armchair, a slightly more formally dressed and bespectacled Razali and Aziza with three children; and finally, a Razali now middle-aged, in a formal suit with heavy horn-rimmed glasses, Aziza still seated, and five children scattered around the scene. The couple had ten births in all, but only five survived. My brother and I had only ever known the young Razali and Aziza.

And Li Saunders? That was Razali, of course. After we left, Razali became known as Li ('who-worked-for') Saunders, and kept the name long after people had forgotten us. For nearly forty years, hidden in the jungle in Peninsular Malaysia, our name had been kept alive in the remote town of Pekan.

'So,' said Aziza, 'welcome home, and be sure to bring your family with you next time!'

The monsoon was thundering on to the roofs of Pekan, making a noise like a drumroll as the Kuantan bus left town. The rain was hitting the puddles so hard a fine mist hung above their surface and the bus ploughed through them like a speedboat.

'Yes, Aziza,' I said to myself. 'I will return. I will.'

But I never did.

2

SCHOOLDAYS

(1961–1969)

After spending our early years running about in the lush Malaysian jungle, my brother and I were confined to a bleak Scottish boarding school so far from Razali and Aziza that we lost one of the languages we grew up speaking. Now we spoke only English. It was heartless, horrible and cold, this new place, this school my father sent us to. The village nearby was famous, not for the archaic, soon-to-be-obsolete school, but for a tiny suspension bridge, the first of its kind, designed in the early 1800s by Thomas Telford.

I was twelve years old, asthmatic, small for my age, brown-skinned and missing our old life in Pekan. Furthermore, eleven-year-old Christopher was better than me at everything, from ping-pong to arithmetic. On top of all that, I had the misfortune to develop allergies and religion at the same time, a coincidence that linked them inextricably in my mind. It happened like this.

Near the school was a walled garden. In north Scotland, walled gardens offer some sort of paradise. Surrounded by windswept moorland and bleak country of bracken and heather, the world behind these walls was a kind of Eden. And within the shelter of this walled garden was an orchard. The orchard had cherry trees. I had never seen cherries in Malaya. They must have looked to me like bushes sprinkled with red sweets. So I tried one.

The following year, I made several more clandestine trips to the walled garden, getting in by climbing a tree next to the wall. I began to notice a mild itching in my mouth after these visits, but at first thought little about this irritation. It was only in the third year that the itching became unbearable and, finally, I connected it with stealing cherries. So began my first religious conviction. There had been no apple or snake in this garden, but it was a deductible truth that I was being punished for stealing the forbidden fruit that *was* on offer. Only God could have been witness to my sin. I had not yet been introduced to the idea that correlation is not causation. As far as I knew, I had stumbled on incontrovertible proof of the existence of God.

At the start of one winter term, a new boy arrived from Switzerland. He was dubbed 'Kana' Kagan because of how he prefaced every utterance with 'I kind of', which with his heavy accent sounded like 'a-kana' to our ears. He had apparently been to some kind of Americanised international school before being sent to Scotland. Kagan was bulkier than me and, in a school where bullies were a constant threat, a bulky friend was a good friend. At his previous school, Kana Kagan had learnt to ski and he promised to show me how. In winter, snow lay heavily around the school except in one spot: the heap of horse dung, which was always steaming hot. It was the kind of school that had horses, and consequently horse-dung heaps.

Kagan took me to the top of the small hill that ended at the steaming dung heap and gave me some basic instruction.

'Ya kana turn your skis downhill.'

The planks thought otherwise, and took me swiftly in the direction of the steaming heap. All I could say was 'Argh!' And then 'No. No! NO!' And then, spitting dung, a final 'Yecht!'

By the time I was thirteen, I had to wear glasses. At first I sat at the back of the class with Fenton, Fleming and Gilmour, a trio of class miscreants. (They probably became a firm of solicitors.) Then, unable to read the blackboard, I moved up from the back rows. The teachers, unaware of my failing eyesight, were under the impression that Saunders was exhibiting a growing interest in their pet subjects. Gilmour showed me how, if I held my thumb, index and middle finger as if holding chopsticks, I could make a small triangular hole through which writing on the blackboard seemed a bit clearer. I was making a crude version of a pinhole camera, but the value of this interesting experiment in optics was lost to me when, even from the front row, even with the chopstick pinhole, I still needed to squint and twist my head. It was obvious the other boys could see things I could not. It was time to start wearing glasses. Although I later acquired the flimsy wire-rimmed type that John Lennon made so popular, the first NHS frames they gave me were more Buddy Holly. I soon became accustomed to wearing these glasses all the time and could barely see without them.

The year 1963 was the year of the Great British Freeze and the Kennedy assassination, and many other things of which I was wholly ignorant. All 1963 meant to me was that this was the year I would play rugby for the first time. We played these outdoor games because our housemaster, 'Chum' Lawson, said that they were 'good for your health'. Furthermore, he continued, 'the game of rugby, hard as it is, will inculcate in you that sense of fair play we pride ourselves on here in this school. I want you to play fair. I want you to *play hard*.'

For my first match, I was conscripted for an inter-house game. I arrived on the field wearing my Buddy Holly specs. It was a horribly cold day. The pitch's turf had recently been turned over by a passing herd of cows, and the icy clods were tinged with frost. I considered how just lying on the ground looked unpleasant, while being made to fall on it was downright repugnant. All the other boys seemed already to be stubbly bearded men, a foot taller than me and bulging with threatening muscles. My future looked unappealing. Then I realised Chum was shouting at me.

'Saunders! You can't wear those here, you clot!'

I spotted a hole in the ground and put my glasses in it. It was a perfect cylinder of a hole, the size and shape of a can of beans, too narrow for a foot to get in. Even if the whole team of boys ran across the hole, my specs would be protected. Plus, I would always be able to find it again because it was located at a spot where two white lines painted on to the grass crossed each other.

My position was scrum half. It was the only place the games-master could find for me. I was half the size of the others, asthmatic and, though he had not realised it, hard of seeing. The scrum half's job is simple: you collect the ball from the back of the scrum and, with an elegant dive, pass it to the fly half or the three-quarter line. Having delivered the ball, you continue to slide through the mud on your tummy and look up as the game races away from you. When it is done well, the pass is beautiful. That was my job.

My enemy was the opposing wing forward, a boy called McKenzie. His job was to spoil the pass. This is how the spoiling was done: scrum half (me) pulls the ball from his side of the scrum, eyes up the field and, with that elegant dive, throws the ball in a graceful arc to the fly half, who passes it on with a swing of his hips. At this point, while I am still flat-bellied on the mud squinting at Fenton, who was selling a dummy and twisting and whirling through the line of plodding forwards, the breath is driven out of my asthmatic body. Wing forward's knees are on my kidneys, an unshaven chin scratching the back of my neck, and a hoarse whisper in my ear:

'Touch that ball again, Saunders, and I'll break your back.'

Chum Lawson was at the other end of the field encouraging the boys.

'Hammer! Hammer! Hammer! Put some *beef* into it!'

Given that I was only little and they were huge, these boys from the other house, I was still groaning as I dragged myself off the ground.

Gilmour ran past muttering, 'Was that McKenzie? Don't worry, I'll get him next time.'

At least, I think it was Gilmour. I couldn't see much without my glasses, so it might have been Fenton. Or Fleming. Or Kagan. I ran around the field squinting and looking for the biggest concentration of blue shapes, our house colours. Then I saw something large and white charging in my direction. Chum was shouting again.

'Tackle! Tackle! Tackle!' I don't think it was a stammer; it was just his way: three repetitions and whatever is required must be done. Or else we were too stupid to understand the instruction the first two times.

'You there! Saunders! Tackle! Tackle! Tackle!'

High tackles, grabbing folk above the waist, were meant to be dangerous, so we were instructed to throw ourselves at their knees, bind their legs together and thus force the player to fall. After that, something was supposed to happen with the ball, what exactly I wasn't too sure, but I did understand I was meant to tackle this big white thing charging at me. I ran at it, and saw a pair of gigantic knees pumping up and down, pistons of solid bone, coarse and hairy and dangerous. I threw myself at them, wrapping my arms round the knees, and as the white thing began to fall I realised I had tackled McKenzie by mistake. It was a bit late to apologise. He twisted as he fell, and this time succeeded in landing on my chest with his knees, his yellow teeth (he had clearly not brushed them that morning) snarling through the contortions of his hateful face.

'I've warned you, Saunders, don't get in my way again, or I'll fuckin' kill you.'

A ruck was forming round us and the ball went to the blue side. Blue and white shapes darted away to another part of the field. McKenzie got up to rejoin the play, grinding his studded heel into my hand as he left.

Chum ran past and boomed, 'Fine tackle, Saunders! *Fine* tackle. Keep it up!' Then he ran on to follow the ball.

Play had now raced up to the other end of the field. Beyond the goalposts was a small chapel, hidden by a copse of holly. Moss-covered gravestones and overgrown gravel paths circled the building. I knew the church was there, just as I knew the goalposts were there, but I could see neither. Nor could I see what the players were up to, since they were now quite far away and everything looked blurred.

Then something hit me square in the chest. Looking down, I saw it was the ball. Without thinking, I bent and clutched it to my heart. Then I began to run, although in what direction I'm not sure, since I wasn't certain whose goal I was now facing. Even before I looked up, I knew my horizon would be filling with white and blue shapes. There would be thirty of them: fifteen opponents in white, fourteen on my side in blue and Chum, all shouting, all running straight at me. I had recently seen a film where charging herds of bison overran a trail of pioneer wagons. It had been carnage. And so was this.

In retrospect, I suppose I experienced a moment of panic. Thirty huge men were charging down the field, all thirty converging on me. What else could I do? I threw the ball in the air and ran away.

When all the noise and shouting died down, I went to look for my glasses, where the white lines crossed at a corner of the field. This corner was now marked with a corner post, and under the post, at the bottom of the post hole, were the remains of my glasses. I think very probably this was the moment I decided to join the school chess club. At least the pain of losing was not so physical.

What a miserable place school was. I hated being so incompetent at games. I hated being unable to see in class. I hated being small and brown-skinned. I hated being asthmatic. On top of it all, my allergies grew in number and consequence. I became allergic to apples, peaches and nuts. I became allergic to poodles, cats and horses. I developed eczema on my legs and arms. I couldn't wait for my parents to visit, which, being divorced, they did separately. But I was horribly self-conscious and easily embarrassed, so couldn't bear it when eventually they did show up. Most of all, I couldn't wait to leave.

When I mucked out the pony stables, it was with rivers of allergic tears, liquid snot and unbearable itching. This Abrahamic god was certainly vengeful. An eye for an eye was all very well, but both my eyes were in allergic purgatory. It all seemed a bit over the top for a few cherries, much more than the Old Testament demanded for similar infringements. It all seemed so unfair.

When Dr McDonald explained that my allergies were simply an inappropriate immune response and that antihistamines could reverse it all, I began to suspect God might not be behind my misery after all. There was a new inhaler for asthma, called Ventolin. If you don't have asthma, you won't know that Ventolin is The Most Amazing Treatment Ever. One minute you are suffocating in fresh air from horse-induced asthma. Then you take two puffs on the inhaler, and in seconds you can breathe again, like a diver coming up for air. Even better, the antihistamines seemed to work well for the allergies.

So, as the good doctor explained, it wasn't punishment; it was biology. Life wasn't like rugby: random, unfair and violent. It was like chess: rational, structured and predictable. This new realisation required a test, an experiment. So, while nobody else was watching, I carefully placed a Bible on the floor. Then I climbed on to a chair next to the book and gently half stepped, half jumped off the chair on to the Bible. Then I pushed a table over to the Bible. (Why I didn't just toe the thing along the floor towards the table, I have no idea. Perhaps it didn't seem respectful.) I climbed on to the chair, then the table. Sucking in a huge breath, I leapt and landed with the full force of my small weight on the holy book.

Looking up, I wondered how long I would have to wait.

3

SEX AND DRUGS AND ROCK CLIMBING

(1970–1972)

When I finally left school, when I escaped, I was still looking up and waiting. Somewhere up there, men were walking on the moon. My mother had remarried and produced another batch of children. We were now an extended family of four boys, two girls, two fathers and one mother.

Kagan and I were now students in London. We had our own (quite separate) lodgings. We were learning to cook beans on toast and how to spend money on beer. We were also learning that in the normal world, the world outside our boarding school, people generally called each other by their first names. Kana Kagan was now Nick, student of medicine. I was trying to come to terms with architecture school.

We still shared ski trips at Nick's family home near Lac Léman. He was still trying to show me how the planks worked. In England, we discovered another new thing: rock climbing. This was going to change our lives, but we didn't know that yet.

In 1969 there was just one climbing shop in London and climbing had yet to become part of the fashion industry. Climbers dressed as appallingly as cavers. In fashion terms, they were more or less cavers above ground. That one shop was the YHA in John Adam Street, a dark and dingy alley leading to Charing Cross station. At the desk there was a fierce old woman in a collared button-down dress.

'Why do you want the climbing department?' she asked severely.

'I … um, I want to go climbing.' Was I threatening to commit some kind of crime?

She gave me a pitying look and extended a yellow cigarette-stained finger, pointing towards a dark stairway that led up several rickety flights to a Dickensian attic. At the top of the stairs, on the other side of the decaying panelled door, was a long tabletop that served as a display for some climbing boots, a helmet and a Pink Floyd LP. Ropes and bits of metal hung from the walls. They looked like parts, parts I could not name, from a precision engineering factory. At the far end of the room was a spotty youth hanging from the ceiling with his feet in nylon slings. He was swinging around quite a bit and had to crane his long neck round to see me. I said I wanted to learn how to climb. The youth climbed down from his contraption and then said:

'You need to buy one of these, a pair of these and a couple of those.'

I later found out I was being sold a climbing harness, a pair of rock-climbing shoes and a steel snap link.

'Go to Avon Gorge and ask someone to climb with you.'

On the way out with my booty, the fierce old woman gave me a suspicious look.

Next day I was under the most forbidding-looking cliff imaginable: grey and vertical for 400 feet. In the near distance was Brunel's Clifton Suspension Bridge. In the car park under the cliff was a tea van. I bought a paper cup of builder's tea and tried to take in the sheer stupidity of what I was doing. A formerly white minivan pulled up beside the tea van and a scruffy man with a badly shaved face got out and stretched his cramped body. He bought himself a cup of the same vile tea I was drinking.

'Well,' I said. 'Um. Hello?'

'Yer?' said Scruffy. His eyes were bloodshot.

'Do you fancy a bit of a climb?'

'S'why I'm here. You climbed before?'

'Oh yes,' I lied. And then added, 'Just a little bit rusty.'

'Kay. What've you got?'

At this point I felt familiar waves of panic surging in. I didn't understand what he wanted. What did he mean, what have you got? Did I look ill? Was I pale or something?

'Excuse me?'

'Gear. Gear, mate. Ropes? Pegs? Nuts? Slings?'

His eyes narrowed, showing less red and a little less tolerance. I put on a sort of apologetic smile and said, 'I've got a sling?'

'S'at all? Right, we'll use my gear and do *Piton Route*.'

'Pitons? I … ah … haven't put in one of those for a while.'

'S'okay, jus' the name of the route.'

And so Scruffy pulled on his climbing shoes and harness and led the way to the bottom of the cliff. The path to the climb now got steeper and it seemed there was a good chance I would hurt myself if I slipped. I was getting the idea that maybe Scruffy was not going to use the rope at all. In time I discovered his name was not Scruffy; it was Dave. I just didn't know that yet, so instead I called him 'Hey, man!' I thought saying 'man' might make me sound a little less posh, just in case this was why he seemed set on frightening me.

'Hey, man! Do you think we should maybe use the rope sometime?'

'We will use the rope … at the start of the effing climb. This is still the path.'

Piton Route, I was soon to discover, is a climb of four pitches. Dave led the first, which very soon became quite difficult. It ended with a traverse, a few horizontal moves above a seemingly vast overhang. I was terrified. I had never done anything like this before. I looked down below my heels where the rock just curled away in the most confusing way. The ground was already a hundred feet below me. I was not comfortable. I inwardly cursed the day I walked into the YHA. I cursed the spotty youth. I cursed the dreadful overhang below my feet.

'I don't think I can do this.'

'Well, if you look up left a bit, you see that little ledge? Keep yer feet low and shuffle along till you can reach that. Then there is a small pocket for yer fingers.'

And in a few moments, I was sitting on the belay ledge next to Dave, feet dangling over the edge.

Back at the car park, I said, 'Hey. That was far out. Thanks, man. That was fantastic.'

'Yer.'

'I ought to say, I was not really telling you the truth. That was actually my first ever climb.'

'Yer, I know … And by the way, you can call me Dave instead of "Hey, man!"'

The following week I persuaded Nick to go to the YHA with me. We met the dangling youth, who said he was going down to Bristol that weekend. We bought twenty karabiners, two ropes, some slings and half a dozen nuts. With full rucksacks we hitch-hiked from the end of the Metropolitan line to Bristol. In those days, it was not unusual to see long-haired (me) and bearded (Nick) youths lining the side of the main roads, thumbs pointing the way.

There are guidebooks with dozens, even hundreds of climbs described in the Avon Gorge, but I didn't know that then. The only climb I knew about was *Piton Route*, because it was the only one I had done. So the weekend was a repeat of the Scruffy Dave thing, except I led the pitches and Nick did the whimpering. It took twenty minutes to talk Nick across the traverse.

'Impossible!'

'You can do it!'

'No. I need to go back. I'll pay for the ropes we leave behind.'

'Really, it's not as bad as it looks.'

Nick was looking down beneath his feet to the ground a hundred feet below.

'I can't do this.'

'Well, if you look up left a bit, you see that little ledge? Keep your feet low and shuffle along till you can reach that. Then there is a small pocket for your fingers.'

At the foot-dangling belay ledge, I pulled out a packet of Player's No.6: the cheapest and meanest cigarettes money could buy. We had spent all our student grant on the ropes and karabiners, so couldn't afford Benson & Hedges, let alone Gitanes or Gauloises. Nick and I smoked the entire packet of cigarettes on that ledge. And that was the beginning of our climbing partnership.

The next climb we tried was technically easier but we got lost in the middle. It really wasn't obvious where the route went next. And we knew that if we chose the wrong way, we would be in trouble. The route was called *Sinister*, probably with good reason. It began to drizzle. Dust on the key foothold turned to mud. I was at the sharp end of the rope and kept slipping down to balance one-footed on this tiny muddy foothold. Drizzle turned to rain.

Then we remembered reading somewhere that escaping from climbs involved something called 'abseiling'. We weren't sure about abseiling, but climbing down the now wet and slippery rocks didn't seem any more appealing. Flat ground seemed awfully far away. Nick was the more intelligent and sensible one in our partnership, so I asked him the obvious question.

'What do you think?'

'Hmm, let me see.' He looked at me as though he had never been asked this question before and then said, very slowly, 'What do I think? ... I think ... that we both think ... that we should not be here.'

The weather had deteriorated into a full-scale summer storm; the rain had now soaked through our clothes. We decided to abandon two of the very expensive nuts we had bought only the day before, rationalising that they were a small price to pay for our lives. We fed the rope through them and did our best to remember how it all worked in the books. Then we slid jerkily down the ropes.

The Youth from the eponymous Hostel Association had been watching our antics with a kind of funereal amusement. He gave us his verdict as we hid from the rain under the awning of the dreadful tea van.

'I'll give you about two weeks.'

'Two weeks? What for?'

'Two weeks to stay alive in the Alps!'

This was cruel but also fair. Our performance had been risible. He was kind not to laugh out loud at us. Like Scruffy Man, Spotty Youth also had a name, but it wasn't Dave. It was Wilmot. Tony Wilmot. The shower passed by, and half an hour later Wilmot climbed up to our abandoned nuts and threw them down to us. He was climbing without rope. He did a lot of that. It was called soloing. Sometimes he did that while smoking cannabis. We all smoked cannabis; we were only just in our twenties, after all. Cannabis came in many colours. There was Nepal Black, a resinous product that had the texture of plasticine. Moroccan Green was mild. Red Lebanese was powdery but very strong. There was also a product called Malawi Laughing Weed. I don't remember what colour that was; it was the sort of stuff that if you did remember the colour, you hadn't smoked it. Wilmot liked them all.

Smoking weed, as we soon discovered, did not always go well with climbing. The week after *Piton Route*, we discovered the nearest climbing to London was at Harrison's Rocks near Groombridge in Sussex. Although only forty feet tall, this long sandstone outcrop was host to hundreds of short technical routes which were either soloed or top-roped. Some of these climbs included the famous Harrison's move, where you jamb your knee in a horizontal crack and try not to dislocate your hip while performing a one-arm press-up.

The Niblick was just such a climb. I had just got to the hip-dislocation move when I noticed the rope was loosely coiled round Nick's feet. There was a dazed expression on his bearded face and I saw, in spite of all the facial hair, his mouth was agape.

24

'I like the word agape,' I told myself. So I repeated it. 'Agape! Agape!'

The rock was now beginning to move. It had become a living thing. I discovered I was doing the Harrison's move on an elephant. Suddenly I wondered if I had been pronouncing 'agape' correctly. I had been rhyming it with 'a grape'.

'It's Greek,' I said to myself. 'So shouldn't it rhyme with sag-happy?' I tried out some alternatives.

'Agg-ap-ee … agg-ap-ay … agg-ap-oo … '

It then came back to me that I was now twenty feet from the ground and no one was holding the other end of the rope. Some small voice, still not terrified about the fall potential, said to me this was not at all as it should be. I shouted down to Nick.

'Um, excuse me?'

'Yah?'

'The rope?'

'Yah? 'bout the rope?'

'Shouldn't you be holding it?'

'Yah. But, man, just look at the trees!'

He was right. The trees had quite suddenly become extremely beautiful, birch leaves twinkling grey and lime green, branches swaying in time to the slight summer breeze. I don't remember how I got down from the climb, but I do remember spending the rest of the day puffing away at the Red Lebanese, watching the dancing birch twigs and occasionally saying the word 'agape'.

It was about this time that in addition to cannabis and climbing we discovered that there were also women. It would have been difficult to put these three very important themes in a hierarchy, but I suppose the fact we spent most weekends climbing gives away the sad truth: girls were the third most important thing in our lives. The day had been filled with the first two, and we were sitting on the sand in front of the brilliant birch when Nick said:

'Hey, man, I've just remembered. There's a party tonight.'

'Oh. Who is it? I mean, where, man?'

'Canonbury. Grania. Her parents are away.'

Grania was eighteen, but more grown-up than any boy I knew. She was tall and wore jeans, flat shoes and a man's tweed jacket. Maybe it was the hormones. Perhaps it was the alcohol. Perhaps it was the remains of the climbing day. Perhaps the fact that it was her party acted as an aphrodisiac. Maybe it was just lust; I'm not sure. Whatever it was, when I glimpsed her across the room through the cigarette smoke, between the talking heads and clinking beer cans, I instantly fell in love. Except the Red Lebanese had left me so tongue-tied that all I could say to Grania when I was able to get close was:

'Ah. Well. I mean.'

'You mean ... what?'

'I mean ... great party, Grania.' I grimaced at my hopeless incompetence.

'Lovely, you have a good time.'

And with a brief smile and the fleetest of glances from her liquid eyes, she turned her lovely back and sailed away across the sea of students.

At least the beer was good. Actually, let me be clear: the beer was normal, but that in itself is already very good. I was making a list, a kind of scale to measure the amount of beer-drunkenness I was experiencing. I called it the 'anaesthetic scale'. So far, I had three levels worked out. I supposed the body goes numb sequentially. The first level was a slight numbing of the tip of the tongue. 'Was that really only level one?' I asked myself. After all, you had probably already halved your chess rating by then. And yet I could not think of a lesser numbness. Then there was a numb nose. That together with the numb tongue usually meant you were slurring your words. Level two, maybe. Level three was numb feet. That meant you were stumbling. With numb feet, it's better not to try to walk.

I had just got around to considering what level four might be when Grania appeared at my side and, glancing towards the stairs with those lovely eyes, led me across the room. She held my hand tight and we pushed through the crowd. I could hardly believe it. Conversation was intense; animated groups argued and spilt beer on the carpet. One man was pointing out the flaws in his opponent's case with a cigarette that was dripping ash. The record player was turned up as far as it would go, but the Blues Breakers were losing the sound war. The noise level was indescribable. But I heard nothing. I only knew that what was happening to me now was new.

Grania led the way out of the room. I said nothing, since that way my useless tongue could do nothing to betray me. I just stared mutely at her lovely back, the tweed jacket and those tight jeans, a blur of brown and blue and tweed. 'My God!' I thought. Had I finally got lucky? Alternatively, had I reached level four in the anaesthetic scale? I was certainly transfixed, my voice silenced, my brain anaesthetised. Was I now merely in a dreamworld?

It was an old house, yellow London Stock bricks on the outside. Architects remember these things. The iron railings from this part of the street had been melted down for guns during the war and had not been replaced since then. By the look of it, neither had the wallpaper. I didn't mind. All I knew was that Grania was leading the way up the stairs. She was leading me by the hand.

There were people sitting on the stairs. I didn't recognise any of them. I supposed they were Grania's friends, drinking and smoking. Some spoke to each other. We stepped over their feet, past the trail of empties. There were more people on the landing. I thought nothing of it. Grania continued to grip my sweaty palm in her strong hand. There was another flight of stairs. 'Hmm,' I thought, 'we are going all the way to the attic!' The house seemed to have grown narrower. There was less room. People were in the way. They were standing on the steps. No longer happily smoking and drinking, these attic people looked slightly distressed and uncomfortable. They were fidgeting; some were hopping from leg to leg. Others were whistling anxiously to themselves.

Grania's grip on my hand was tighter now. At the top of the stairs was a door. So this is where Grania was leading me. She pushed it open. It led to a very small room. It was a loo. On the loo seat there was a man asleep, head on his knees, trousers round his ankles. I could see he had a beard. A sort of blond beard. A beard that looked vaguely familiar. His mouth was agape and he was snoring the snore of one who has finally achieved level four on the anaesthetic scale.

'Now,' Grania said, 'is this your friend?'

'No. Absolutely not.'

It was the truth. For in that moment Nick Kagan was most definitely not my friend.

In the summer of 1972 I took an architecture job in Japan for almost no money. These days we call that an internship. It would be a year before I saw my non-friends and family again.

4

SHIP AHOY!

(1973)

The architect's office was in Shibuya and I found cheap digs in Waseda, a student district. The time flew by. I could witter on at length here about Tokyo, Kyushu, Kyoto and Nagoya, but that would only distract from this story. This story is about my life as a failed sailor.

My time in Tokyo was coming to an end. Soon I would be going home to London and resuming my studies. It was simply a question of how. The obvious journey was via China and Russia. The Trans-Siberian Railway appealed to me but was expensive and I had no money. So, what to do?

To make ends meet, I found a job as a watchman in Yokohama, Tokyo's seaport. The job involved wearing a grey suit with a Mandarin collar. Most foreign crews in Yokohama spoke English but not Japanese, and so for a month my job was to board the visiting ships and, when necessary, call for a taxi, ambulance or whatever minor request needed converting from broken English to pidgin Japanese. It was a surprisingly easy job. I hung out on the ship's bridge, chatting to the helmsman or first mate or whichever matelot was in charge. I drank tea continuously. And on every ship, I asked if I could work my passage back to Europe.

During the days when there was no work, I wandered through the port, the cranes and silos looming huge in the drizzle and mist.

Sometimes rats ran across the derrick rails or splashed through the oily puddles right in front of me. I could hear them every night in the dormitory I shared with the other watchmen. Creatures ran across the corrugated iron roof and down through the hollow shed walls in the night. There was always a smell of shipping oil and fermenting grain. I was not to know it then, but all ports smell of rotting grain and diesel oil, a smell I came to love. It was the common factor in all the ports I was ever to visit. Even now, half a century later, the smell of an industrial port fills me with a desire to chuck it all in and run away to sea.

The ship that came to my rescue was called the *Northern Frost*, a 4,000-tonne freezer: a type affectionately known as a banana boat. The ship had a crew of twenty-two but was designed for thirty-two. The men were Filipinos, Indonesians and Moroccans, but the officers were Greek. The chief engineer spoke English.

'Yes, okay, I will ask the captain. If he says yes, we sail tomorrow. Can you leave tomorrow?'

'*Efharistó … Efharistó polí!*' I had just looked up these words in my Collins useful phrasebook. 'Thanks a lot!'

The chief was in charge of everything below decks, assisted by the first and second engineer, who spent most of their time in the workshop playing with lathes and drills. There were two oilers helping them. They were from Agadir: Hassan and Ali. They went round the engine room squirting oil at anything that moved and quite a lot that did not. And at the bottom of this hierarchy was the one and only wiper: me. I was literally the oily rag. Ali became my friend on the boat; more of him later.

The *Northern Frost* made money for its German owners by being understaffed, being registered in Cyprus and taking last-minute contracts. As we left Yokohama for Europe, a new contract came in and we headed for Australia. There was a glut of cheap beef there, apparently. It was June and since I didn't need to arrive in London before September, I wasn't worried. Yet.

The boat steamed to the South China Sea, which the Malaysians call Laut Selatan. I knew this because Pekan lies on its shores. After passing the Philippines, we edged through the eastern tip of the Indonesian archipelago and on to Darwin. I did not see much of that passage. I toiled in the engine room and came up for air twice a day. The marine diesel engine was the size of a locomotive. I tended the beast. Its heartbeat was a constant presence: throbbing, grinding, clattering, banging and insanely loud. I wiped oil from the corners of its mouth. It was 40° Celsius in the boiler room. I worked in shorts. Sweat ran into my eyes. Over the course of each shift, I would become deafened to the noise until I emerged on deck as it ended. Then the silence was shocking. And even the equator felt cool.

After the Celebes, we had two days in Darwin, where the crew had shore leave. Ali said it was not worth visiting Darwin, so I went to look for surf and popped into town for a beer. Ali was right, as usual. Darwin was awful. The surfers on the beach were insufferably arrogant. And when I asked the taxi driver to pick up an aboriginal woman who was hitch-hiking, the driver asked why I would want to do that. My impression was that the town was filled with arrogant bigots. When Cyclone Tracy destroyed the town on Christmas Day that year, it made me rethink my views on divine retribution.

Not all my memories of Darwin were bad. I soon discovered that with this kind of vessel, transporting sides of beef had an advantage. The shipping industry allows for a certain amount of spoilage during loading, and the first thing to go was one of the beef crates. Now of no value to its owners, the crate had become trash and was moved to the kitchen store. Thereafter we dined on steak.

A few days later we sailed into Broome. In 1973 this town of 2,000 souls was the largest settlement in an area the size of Europe. There was a main street of clapboard houses with wild-west sidewalks and a bar with swing doors. In the harbour was a Japanese pearl-fishing fleet. I don't remember much else of Broome: the beer was weak and when I swam in the sea I must have brushed against some coral because one of my legs developed a wound that took weeks to heal.

After Broome came Fremantle, Adelaide and Melbourne. The most memorable thing was crossing the Great Australian Bight: the 1,250-mile bay on the south side of the continent. In this Sisyphean sea, each wave was another mountain for the boat to climb. For days the *Northern Frost* bobbed like a cork, crawling up steep faces of water many times its size, then taking a stomach-churning slide down the back of these giant waves before repeating the whole terrifying cycle, the ship creaking as it climbed.

The bridge was at least twenty metres above the Plimsoll line, yet we could look up and see waves bearing down on us. This meant, I reasoned, that the waves were taller than the ship, or at least taller than the bridge. I felt quite ill. We all did – almost all, because the first mate was the only man (we had no women on board) who was sufficiently well to work. His secret was dry toast and beer. We weren't officially allowed beer at sea, but someone had to steer the boat.

After four days of this, I became so sick I lay on the deck near the stern where, sheltered from the wind and spray, it was safest to vomit, and where I began to lose the will to live. I offered to cast my diaries and my atheism into the sea if only the rolling would stop. It did. My prayers were answered. Melbourne hove into view.

As well as possessing a perfect natural anchorage, a sea loch protected by peninsular arms and a narrow opening, Melbourne was, at the time, the second-largest Greek city in the world. Only Athens had more Greeks. So, I don't suppose it was too big a surprise when our Greek cook failed to return to the boat at the end of our two days there.

'Where are we going now?' I asked the first mate.

'Tasmania.'

'Really?'

'They have langoustine there.'

Amazingly, one of the langoustine crates was also slightly damaged during loading. Now we alternated between steak and lobster at dinner.

Crossing the Bass Strait to Tasmania had involved another hideous shift in the engine room. To calm my nerves, I unpacked the reel-to-reel tape player I'd bought in Japan from my sea chest and listened to a mixture of Beethoven and early Cream. 'Rollin' and tumblin', Ali said, looking out of the porthole at the wind and waves, and added that this kind of blues was really North African music, not European.

I woke to the gentle throb of the engine. It was the only noise. No rolling beer cans on the floor; no crashing waves on the hull side. Looking through the porthole, a scene from rural England was scrolling past, like something from a magic lantern: fields and trees and cows. It was July, the Antipodean winter, and this was Tasmania, the southernmost part of Australia. And still the fields were green. One cow looked up at us in brindled curiosity. The rest of the herd continued munching their herbaceous breakfast.

Ali said it would be interesting to look at the Plimsoll line on the boat.

'Why?'

'Because in sweet water we are lower than in the sea.'

'Ah, so that's why the cows seem so high.'

'Eh? What are you asking? You are crazy, my friend!'

But it was sort of true. We did float lower in the fresh water than in the denser salt sea. The portholes of the lower cabins, where the deckhands and oilers and wiper lived, seemed closer to the cows than expected.

After Launceston, the *Northern Frost* sailed back to Melbourne. A new cook had been flown out from Athens. After that, we sailed to Sydney and its spectacular harbour entrance. I stood on the foredeck, blue-lipped and cold, salt wind blowing my long hair into my eyes, as we rounded the Hornby Lighthouse into Sydney harbour and the white sails of the opera house slid into view. As an architecture student, the new opera house should have been foremost in my mind, but I recalled reading what Le Corbusier said to the Architectural Association School of Architecture in 1953: 'I do not want to talk to you about architecture. I detest talk about architecture ... architecture is something to be done, not talked about.' Like sex and drugs and rock climbing. Often described as a masterpiece of modern architecture, the opera house as a building neither interested nor impressed me. It's certainly impressive as a piece of sculpture, but not as a work of architecture. In 1956 Jørn Utzon had imagined the opera house as a collection of billowing sails. Unfortunately, the sails of this ship, being concrete, don't fill with the wind. So if, in good design, form follows function, this was a case of bad design. Utzon had the idea of making a concrete metaphor for the harbour, paying no respect to how well the building would work for those inside. In 1956, architecture had fallen into the world of fashion. Conceptual art had taken precedence over use. The metaphor had feet of clay.

'Why do you not like it?' asked Ali.

'It is because from the inside you don't see the outside. Architecture has to be lived in. It's lovely to go past on a ship, but everyone says the acoustics are terrible. You know, Ali, the best part of automobile design is when you lift up the hood and look at the engine.'

'I don't understand, but I think maybe you are crazy, my friend!'

Jørn Utzon's masterpiece might have left me cold, but the sweeping panorama of the harbour and the grey skies, so heavy and pregnant with rain, held my attention. I gazed, lost in admiration and trying hard to remember the last time I was there, and what my grandmother might look like.

I hadn't seen Baba, my Russian grandmother, since I was two years old. I had one early memory, an old woman showing me a peanut. She split it in half, and holding up the part with the germ said:

'This is Santa Claus; this is sled.'

It must have been the beginning of the language phase, because it's my earliest word memory.

So, obtaining leave from ship for two days, and armed with Baba's address, I walked down the gangplank. The chief engineer wished me luck.

'You miss boat, I send you things in town,' Ali said.

'I'll be back tomorrow.'

'Sure thing.' Ali gave me a big wink. He had a weird, lopsided grin on his face. 'Now you are *real* sailor!'

'No, you got it wrong. This *really is* my grandmother.'

'Sure thing. Bring back one girl for me too!'

'No. Really.' But it was hopeless. Ali and the rest of the crew were determined not to believe me.

Balmain, Sydney. In 1973 it was in the early stages of its gentrification. My grandmother had moved there when it was still cheap. She had no choice. Her story had not been a happy one so far. She had fled Siberia in the late 1920s, bringing her children from various spouses with her, first to Harbin, then Shanghai, and finally Hong Kong, where she set up home with Pop. Pop, Ilya Kurya Popov, was a deep-sea diver from Astrakhan. They arrived in time for the Japanese invasion and occupation, which ran from 25 December 1941 to 15 August 1945 and explains why my mother still speaks a little Japanese as well as Cantonese and, of course, Russian.

In the 1950s there was a scheme in Australia to encourage immigration. Baba and Pop bought into it. They started a farm, but after a few hard years, Pop ran off with his Greek lover. Baba was left with the farm and debts. The bank foreclosed on her and she moved with her remaining child, Maria, now grown up, to the cheapest area of Sydney, by the docks. There she made her living as a charlady, slowly paying off the small mortgage she had on her tiny house by pushing mops and cleaning kitchens.

A taxi dropped me in front of a row of small two-storey houses. I stood on the pavement, address in one hand, overnight bag in the other, my new Nikon camera draped round the shoulders. It felt like the middle of nowhere. There was a rickety front fence and a tiny front garden. The house was small. A bit ragged. Paint on the door was peeling. I knocked.

Nothing.

I knocked again, half expecting that I would now have to find my way back to the docks. It wasn't far, as the name of Baba's street implied: Ballast Point Road. Even so, I was alone and didn't relish the prospect. Then I heard a shuffling noise. The door opened a fraction. An eye and half a face appeared at chest height.

'No camera today!' And the door slammed shut.

I knocked again.

'No camera! Not buy camera!'

'Stop! I'm NOT selling cameras.'

'Not buy camera. Not!'

'But I'm your grandson,' I said, pushing the camera behind my back.

'Not buy camera, not buy gransen. Not buy nothing!'

'No, no, listen … wait … your daughter … '

'*Nyet. Nyet! NYET! Ya nichigo ne hoche.*'[1]

'Raiza … your daughter … '

'*Shto vi kazali?*'[2]

'I am Raiza's son.'

'*Da?* Raiza?'

And suddenly the door opened. There she was, a little old woman, the very image of what my mother would be like in thirty years, what I would look like in fifty years. I was looking through time's window into my future.

'My son! My son!' She began weeping real Russian tears as she clutched me to her.

'Actually, I'm your grandson,' I said, but it made no difference.

'My son! My son!'

In the kitchen, she made me sit and watch as she made tea and sliced bread. She was arthritic. Her movements were jerky, and to cross from one side of the room to the other, she first turned to face her target. Then, with eyes fixed on the landing zone, she staggered across the room with arms outstretched until she reached the next table and could pause for a rest. In this way, traverse by traverse with

---

1   'No. No! NO! I don't want anything.'

2   'What did you say?'

one item per journey, tea, bread and butter, and cheese were assembled on the small table beside me. I was not allowed to help, because apparently you cannot go to your Russian grandmother and not be pampered. She pulled up a chair that seemed alarmingly close to collapse and sat across the table from me.

An open bottle of Guinness was already on the table, and she poured this into half a glass of milk.

'Doctor say I need Gyin-ness for bones. Is iron drink!'

Over the next few hours we sat and drank tea and milk-Guinness and she told me a little of her life. I could not follow all of it: her pronunciation was strange, and the story somewhat rambling. At one point she apparently asked me if I agreed that she had been very bad. I wasn't sure what she had done, so I said yes. I found it easier to understand that while Lenin had been some kind of saint, Stalin was Satan. I found it curious the way Russian peasants replaced one iconology with another.

Slowly we ploughed through the great events of the twentieth century and her role in them until she got to the part where Pop ran off to Los Angeles, at which point she gave me some pertinent advice.

'You not marry Greek women. Greek women no good!' It seemed a good time to call Mum.

'So, shall we go down to the Post Office and call Raiza?'

They had not spoken for twenty years. My mother had developed some kind of agoraphobia and had barely left her house for ten of those years. I fed coins into the slot and soon a surprised Raiza could be heard laughing and crying in Russian at the other end.

Next morning I said a tearful goodbye to Baba. I was never to see her again. Two weeks later my mother left her home in Bayswater for the first time in a decade and flew to Sydney. Before that, the *Northern Frost* sailed from Sydney harbour and I waved goodbye to Utzon's sculpture.

'Do we sail to Europe past Cape Town?' I asked.

'Our next port is Panama, then we go home!' said the chief engineer.

After Sydney there was Rockhampton, on the Gold Coast; I don't remember much about that except there were mangrove swamps. Four days later we were in Fiji, pulling into Suva harbour on a Tuesday for, I was told, just four hours and only to take on water and fuel for the Pacific crossing.

To me Fiji was some kind of mythical island paradise. Heard of in passing conversations, glimpsed in the folk stories of others. Independent for just three years, the colonial types who had stayed on were wandering around in sarongs, identifiable from the socks they wore with their sandals. The British had found Fijians so laid-back, I was told they brought Indians in to run the islands' micro civil service. Later, this was to cause considerable friction on the island, but in 1973 the situation appeared more than relaxed. No one seemed interested in manual labour, so it was Thursday before we had sufficient supplies to steam out of paradise.

Looking back on the receding archipelago, the afternoon clouds marking each island, I found myself next to Ali.

'This really *is* the island of the lotus eaters,' I said.

'*Mehveh?*'

'*Mehveh?*' I replied.

'*Mehveh*. It mean, "what are you say?"'

'Oh. Well. Lotus … the reason they don't work is they don't need to. To live, they can pluck fruit from the trees and sleep under the sun. Fiji is the island of lotus eaters. It is a story from the *Odyssey*.'

'Aw-Di-Zeus? Yes. Arabic story. I know.'

'Arabic?'

'But lotus is not the reason we wait days.'

'Eh?'

'*Une manifestation*. Strike. Is politician. Is too many politician.'

As usual, Ali had seen what I could not, that the Melanesian and Indian communities were already beginning to break apart.

We crossed the equator in dead calm, but steaming along at fifteen knots there was some kind of pressure wave at the bow on which a school of dolphins rode for days, occasionally leaping under the bow rail. And to my dying day I will also remember that a lone albatross did the same thing in the air, surfing the wind wave behind the bridge.

Oddly, the air was cool on the equator, and Ali and I were not certain the navigation officer knew what he was doing. Perhaps we had sailed south and were now steaming to Tierra del Fuego. We didn't ask. That was not what oilers and wipers do. After a week, there were birds on the southern horizon.

'Is Galapagos,' said Ali. We were on our mid-morning break. The albatross had left us that day. There was still the school of dolphins playing around the bow. The ocean was so still it looked solid. We leant over the bow looking at the porpoises and talked about life back home. Ali told me about his life in Agadir.

'And do you also have drug problems at home?' I asked.

'Oh no! Drugs no problem at all.' He smiled. 'Is like this. You go to drug store.'

'Yes?'

'Man say, what kind of drug you want? You not know? I show you!'

'Eh?'

'He show you back room. There is man crying. An' there is man laughing. An' there is man thinking. An' there is man sleeping. An' he say to you … what kind of man you want to be? Easy, you see. No drug problem in Agadir.'

A few days later we joined the ship queue at Panama. There were fifty ships in the queue but in the three days we waited we never saw Panama and barely saw the other ships, since this was a queue controlled by radio, and we were anchored over the horizon far from land. The other ships in our queue dotted the horizon. The ship's doctor gave us all yellow fever jabs. And then there was the canal. Tug boats and then a diesel locomotive dragged our 4,000-tonne vessel through the narrow channel. On the far side, in the Atlantic, was the Bay of Limón and Cristóbal harbour.

Saladi was steward on the ship. While the crew ate in the canteen, Saladi served the officers in the mess. He was constantly trying to get into the pants of the young sailors, and had tried his luck, without success, on both Ali and myself. Saladi's best friend was George. So, when Saladi and George were left on watch while the rest of the crew went ashore, I should have understood something was afoot.

The streets were lined with palm trees and I followed the Greek sailors, somehow attaching myself to a group that included the first mate. Since the Great Australian Bight, he had grown a magnificent moustache. We arrived at a whitewashed hacienda built in the colonial Baroque style of the Spanish empire. Through the portico were garden courtyards and wide eaves over the verandas giving shade from the tropical sun and rain. A couple of rather blousy-looking women were draping themselves over the veranda railings. I said to the first mate:

'This place looks just like a bordello, eh? Ha ha!'

I must have been a very naive twenty-three-year-old, because only at this point did it dawn on me that the ship's company had come ashore for what sailors had always done. Not only did this lovely building *look like* a bordello, it *was* a bordello. I had no difficulty making my excuses since the first mate and his friends were focused on one thing only. I left the hacienda and found a cheap restaurant with a telephone. I ordered what turned out to be a very fine mug of excellent Panamanian coffee and called home. Mum was gone, on her way from Bayswater to visit Baba. She was already in Australia.

'Not bad for an agoraphobic!' I said to my brother. 'Whatever will she do next?'

'When are you coming home?'

'Couple of weeks.'

When I returned to the *Northern Frost* after lunch, Saladi and George were making Greek coffee, which they prepared on a bed of fine sand over the stove.

'Yes please,' I said.

Sipping the delicious, sweet muddy liquid, I asked:

'Do they always do this here? I mean, I didn't see anything like this in Australia.'

'Panama,' Saladi explained, 'is where the Atlantic and Pacific ships cross. You understand?'

'Not really.' And after a few seconds of trying to grasp his meaning, I tried another question.

'When do you think you will be home?'

'After this we unload in United States, then home.'

'Oh. Oh well. Okay.' The voyage was getting longer and longer.

After Panama, and sailing through the Caribbean, there was Jacksonville (Florida), Wilmington (Delaware), and then New York and Boston. Boston harbour was without a shadow of doubt the finest port I ever sailed into, fed by the Charles River and the Mystic River. There were yachts sailing along the waterfront, where towering office blocks soared into the cloudy sky. Glaciers calving icebergs into the sea would not have been more spectacular. We had two days in Boston. Ali came back from shore leave love-struck.

'How did you meet this girl? I assume it *was* a girl. Yes? No?'

'You help me write this letter?' he said, holding up a piece of paper.

'You've already written it.'

'Many mistakes, you make good?'

It was his first letter in English, each character printed out with painstaking effort. It began:

'This is one beautifur day. I am think of you all day … '

'Ali, it is perfect. If she doesn't like this, she doesn't deserve you.'

We had nearly finished offloading our cargo; just one more port and we would be finished. We should be on our way home pretty soon.

'When will we be in Europe?' I asked, wondering if the journey across the Atlantic would deliver me to England by the start of term.

'Our last port is Montreal, then we go home!'

But it wasn't and we wouldn't. En route to Montreal I finally plucked up the courage to ask the captain what the real itinerary was.

'After Montreal, we go to Mexico. And then surely we will drive to Europe.'

I was not so sure, and in any case it was September. I was already late for the next term. It was time to go home.

When we got there, I was too preoccupied to take in much of Montreal. My flight gave me a couple of days spare in which I visited the site of the 1967 Exposition, an architectural fair featuring many of the buildings that had become familiar to me as a student. In my angst, I could not take in what I was looking at.

I rang home again.

'She's in Sydney again.'

'Again? What do you mean, again?'

'She went to Los Angeles.'

'What? Why?'

'She went to find Pop. He was washing dishes in a Los Angeles hospital.'

'Wha … ?'

'His hands were raw with the soda.'

'My goodness. That's sad. How about his Greek wife?'

'She died. He's been alone for years.'

'Crumbs!'

'Mum has taken him to Sydney!'

'Crikey! Has the world gone mad?'

'No, just your mum.'

'No, I divorce her. It is "your mum" now.'

Three weeks later I was on Mum's doorstep, rucksack parked on the step beside me. It had been a year and a half since I was last here. In the meantime I had been halfway round the world and so had Mum. She opened the door, saw it was me and, continuing the conversation we had been having when I left in the spring of 1972, marched without a backward glance towards the kettle.

I ended up a month late for the autumn term. Ali sent my sea chest from Montreal. It arrived at the docks in November. I had a couple of postcards from my friend and then the correspondence petered out.

Baba and Pop saw out their final days in Balmain, passing away within a few months of each other. I have no doubt there were fiery Russian word-wars to the end. I wrote in my diary, with apologies to Samuel Beckett:

> *To the lifelong promised land*
> *of the nearest crematoria,*
> *with his Pavla hand in hand,*
> *love it is at last leads Ilya Kurya.*

I caught up with Nick over a beer or two. While I had been in Japan, he had spent six months in New Zealand.

'Much happened while I've been away?'

'Not much. You heard about Wilmot?'

'No?'

'He died in Avon … soloing.'

'God … '

We sat in silence for a while, not knowing what to say. I sipped a bit more beer. Nick scratched inside his pants. I took no notice; he had never been much troubled by the norms of English social behaviour. The incident in Grania's house was just one example of very, very many. But now he looked decidedly unconcerned about the people watching. He told me that something had changed his life.

'What's that?'

'New Zealand!'

'Eh?'

'Don't need to fit in … I have found a country where they are all like me.'

'Crikey! Some country.'

I was about to lose Kana Kagan, my first climbing partner and oldest friend, to New Zealand.

5

LONDON CALLING

(1973–1979)

It was another year or so before Nick emigrated. Meanwhile, being students with little cash, we explored climbing in London as an alternative to travelling to North Wales, Bristol or Groombridge. One of our favourite venues was the Camden canal system.

Beginning at Colebrooke Row in Islington, for the five miles the canal took to run down to the Limehouse Basin, brick walls along the towpath provided as fine an afternoon's outing as was then possible for a climber to find in the capital. There were frequent public houses. In winter the sun warmed the south-facing brickwork. And there we could escape, for a short while, the continual bombardment of London's traffic noise.

Most people brought their dogs and children; we brought climbing shoes and gymnast's chalk. Everybody brought loose change for beer. We saw few other climbers there, though we did meet a couple of East End miscreants: George 'The Greek' Constantinides and his friend Stevie Haston. They were seven years younger than me, but were streetwise in a way that exposed my naivety. I didn't even know the right terminology. Pointing at one problem with a nasty landing, Stevie said:

'And you need a spotter for that route.'

'What is a spotter?'

'Victor, you are so ignorant it hurts.'

The canals worked best if we had our bikes with us but the nearest Underground station was The Angel, where architects Rock Towns-end had created a monstrously large development in a flashy speculative style. Descending the tree-shaded steps to the towpath, where brightly painted narrowboats sat motionless as swans in the ink-black water, it was another world. The winter sun freckled the water. Behind the boats, a tunnel made a perfect oval with its own reflection. Beyond it, the canal led peacefully to King's Cross, Camden and eventually, I supposed, Manchester.

From the steps down to the water, one could walk east under two road bridges, past the back gardens of terraced houses, past City Road basin and on to Wenlock basin, where developers had recently built a mini-docklands in place of the Victorian warehouses that once lined London's canal system.

Coots and ducks fished here, while young men (but no women) angled for sprats. I never saw the boys catch anything. Occasionally a school of kayaks splashed past, which can't have helped. The retaining walls on this stretch of the canal were a reminder of Grania's house: yellow London Stocks, a brick that did not age as gracefully as the red bricks of north-west London. Soot and grime turns the reds to chestnut, but the yellow bricks become dirty brown. Nevertheless, the wall was a suntrap. The yellow-brown wall by Wenlock basin was the first you came to just high enough for brick-edge bouldering. The first climb, or problem, was formed by a dislocation in the wall, where new mortar had been unevenly keyed into the old. A brick hole jug with a little sand under the fingertips and a small undercut overlap allowed a long reach to a sharp-edged top. The trick was to avoid swinging out and off, like a barn door. You had to use the outside of your left foot and inside of the right. Years later I heard this move called an Egyptian.

By the next bridge was a solid staircase edged with Staffordshire Blue engineering bricks. The stairs led up to street level and enclosed a twenty-foot corner. The brickwork corbelled in a bit at fifteen feet, making a slight overhang. The key to this climb was a move akin to doing the splits to get past the overhangs. It was called *Magician* and topped out at the delightful Narrowboat public house. It is a Stevie Haston route, and the distinct possibility of a very hard landing on those hard Staffordshire Blues made it one that required a spotter.

Under the towpath itself was a duct carrying electric cabling, with loose-laid paving slabs covering the duct. The pavers clinked under the wheels of bicycles, giving ample warning to pedestrians and anglers of their approach. Sometimes cyclists were taken by surprise by the climbers. I remember watching Nick fall off *Magician* as a cycle shot into view from under the bridge. The sight of a falling medical student haloed by clouds of chalk was evidently so interesting that the cyclist forgot to steer, and pedalled straight into the water.

Not far past The Narrowboat was one of the city's hidden architectural gems: a furniture factory and, separated by a small yard, a private house for the factory owner. On the canal-side the building was defensively bland, merely a panel edged all round with a thin line of glass obviously designed with vandals in mind. All you could see at first was silver preformed aluminium sheeting. It barely stopped us in our perambulation. But I said to Nick, 'Look carefully. That detailing. The work of a modern master.'

I explained why I thought it was so good. The architects were Benson and Forsyth. Sadly, because of the defensive nature of the facade, we couldn't see the interior, the interplay between light and structure and detail that characterises the work of good designers.

We strolled on, looking for more climbs. Opposite us, across the water, was a renovated warehouse. The four storeys of glazed windows once provided local youths with target practice, and the rehabilitation of the building was one of the few signs of a sensible anti-vandal development policy from Islington Council.

Further downstream, iron railings replaced the canal's retaining wall; great drools of rose and cotoneaster overhung their spikes.

Tiny wavelets from the mallards reflected sunlight on to the under-surface of Victorian bridges that offered climbable features: pillars, corners and crack-riven walls.

Opposite the De Beauvoir estate there was a dry-cleaning works discharging liquids and belching steam across the canal. Here the path entered the wilds of Hackney, leaving Islington's genteel private waterside gardens behind. Trees had been planted in front of the De Beauvoir wall, casting shade where a yellow-brick traverse led to a brick-arched bridge. This wall was almost twenty-five feet high and leant back slightly. Balance was at a premium. In the centre of the soot-stained brickwork, about eight feet from the ground, was a small hole with the diameter of a little finger. The hole was halfway to a narrow sloping ledge, which was itself halfway to the rounded coping at the top. There were no other holds except for rugosities here and there: small imperfections in the old brickwork, which a climber could tiptoe on, feet greasing off the hold. That was all there was to it: a hole and a ledge and some smears. Yet it was a beautiful little climb, combining balance and strength. It was another of Stevie's, called *Logician*.

After *Logician* and the De Beauvoir estate there were more industrial backwaters. A nest of gasometers on the far side of the water, including a large one built in the 1950s with latticework pillars, functional and ugly. Its neighbour was a smaller two-tier Victorian design with iron pillars cast into Doric columns. When the cylinders were down, the columns and ring beams caught the sunlight like a surreal sculpture.

On its way to Victoria Park, the towpath turned leafy. There were more bridges with light dancing on their curved underbellies. In Victoria Park itself, little children played football, their adults threw frisbees and starlings kept up their metallic chatter. This section was terminated by the Old Ford locks, where there was a cottage, the lock-keeper's house that sported a green-edged sign: 'No swimming here.' As if anyone would.

Round the corner from the sign, buried in buddleia, was the back of The Palm Tree. The pub was the last survivor of a terrace that had been flattened by the Luftwaffe, standing in a derelict little park that would later be grassed and planted with rowans that never looked happy to be there. A decade or so later, as climbing changed, a nearby industrial building was turned into a climbing gym where muscle-bound youngsters with matchstick legs would dangle slothfully from the ceiling. But in the 1970s, the building was a youth centre for canal-based watersports.

Beyond The Palm Tree, the scenery reverted to back gardens for the first time since Islington, some full of flowers, some overgrown with convolvulus. The climbing eye was drawn to a wall of decaying Portland stone set raggedly in lime mortar: a hundred feet of crumbling traverse, which usefully culminated at tables and benches outside The New Globe pub and its real ales, pub food and enthusiastic landlord. These days, you catch your first sight of the nursery-school geometry of the Canary Wharf building that appeared as Margaret Thatcher neared her political end, its simple-minded monolith completely dominating a skyline once punctuated only by the steeples of Wren and the towers of Hawksmoor. I had little sympathy for its bankrupt owners or the bankrupt system that put it there.

Sometimes, when alone, I would continue down past Limehouse basin to see St Anne's Limehouse, in my humble opinion one of the finest examples of English architecture ever created. And then, getting really excited, I would continue to cycle round the rest of the Hawksmoor churches in the East End. I could not imagine a better way to spend my time away from the drawing board: exploring hidden London, climbing intricate and interesting problems and then filling my soul with Nicholas Hawksmoor's wonderful obsession with mass, sheer mass.

When Nick finally moved to New Zealand, I found myself living in Stockwell, in a terrace that had been zoned for redevelopment by the local council. The buildings had not been scheduled for demolition for another two years and they had been invaded by students and recent graduates eager not to let good housing go to waste. I was invited to join the commune.

My housemates were mostly architecture students, would-be builders. They practised their art by ripping the plasterboard from most of the walls to reveal a space like a bizarre stage set. The moment you entered the house, you could trace the stairwell from basement to roof. Every joist strut and column was exposed, and the house took on the appearance of a construction drawing. In the commune we were all supposed to be comrades, and so everybody took a turn at cooking as well as mending the roof, chimney stacks or drains. Housework never seemed to find a place on our rota.

In one of those odd little coincidences life offers, Stevie Haston lived in the same terrace. Stevie's house was a bit more civilised than mine: there were more walls between the rooms, for a start. Yet even there it was considered rather un-communal to spend each weekend climbing when slates needed replacing. Each evening, while the others in his household held meetings, Stevie was pushing weights and adding to his already enormous biceps. Even in those days, he was not the sort of person you would want to fight.

Our respective communities took an exceptionally dim view of our plan to disappear for several months in winter to climb in the Bernese Oberland. I further deepened the blot on my copybook by a minor oversight while shopping in Brixton market for a farewell curry. I thought I was buying lamb, but apparently the meat was old goat, and the people in my house turned out to have more conservative tastes than they thought they had.

In preparation for that first winter Alpine season, I had taken to walking everywhere on tiptoe. This was supposed to strengthen my front-pointing calf muscles. To allow my heels to touch the ground was failure. With a briefcase pinch-gripped in each hand to strengthen my forearms (I never used the handle), I staggered round the streets of Stockwell on tiptoe with aching forearms and calf muscles, drawing no more than the usual sidelong glances. I was just another Stockwell eccentric. It makes you wonder what plans the other Stockwell eccentrics were hatching.

Stevie and I took the project very seriously. We had designed and constructed a two-man big-wall tent. The original mock-up had been made from sheets of polythene and sticky tape. The two of us sat inside the tent with our rucksacks, while our housemates looked on disapprovingly. We experimented with three different types of stove and tiptoed up Brixton Hill under huge rucksacks with ten days of food and beer. There were no plastic boots in the 1970s. Our leather Galibier Makalu double boots were loose and bendy and made tip-toeing difficult. We practised front-pointing up the decaying brick-work of our houses. More disapproval. There was so much general disapproval I couldn't understand why the communards weren't actually pleased to see us go to Switzerland. But they weren't. I think they liked their friends to stay at home where they could disapprove of them in person.

THE EIGER (WINTER 1978–79)
Stechelberg is a tiny hamlet at the head of the Lauterbrunnen valley. There was a co-op, post office and hotel. There was also the Natur-freundehaus, a kind of hostel. We were as far from Brixton as it was possible to be. In summer, Stechelberg is lush with flowers and those alpine herbs you see on Swiss cough sweets. In summer, there are tinkling brooks and cowbells, small birds warbling and insects buzzing. But in winter, the valley is so deep the sun does not reach the hostel. This was our base for the winter of 1978–79. We had a couple of tries to climb the Eigerwand. The first was a failure, but Stevie and I now knew we could complete the climb. It hadn't been Haston's first attempt to climb the big one. He started up the 1938 route alone when he was seventeen years old, but his rucksack strap broke on the second icefield and he turned back.

'Did it really break?' I asked Stevie.

'I would have cut it if it hadn't.'

We spent ages struggling up the climb in deep snow. There was a twenty-foot cornice overhanging the Swallow's Nest. Once there, the weather turned bad and we waited another day before committing ourselves. We had just decided to abseil off when I noticed a tiny patch of blue sky. Stevie confirmed the patch was definitely blue and without a word we agreed to wait until the next morning.

The second icefield had a six-inch layer of powder over iron-hard ice. By the time we reached Death Bivouac, our axes and crampons were blunt. We teetered across the ice, grateful for the training we'd done tiptoeing round Brixton. The Waterfall Pitch, an off-width crack in the Ramp, was so choked with powder we had to tunnel through it.

In winter you find very little old gear except where the ground is too steep to take snow or ice. All the pegs in the magnificently exposed brittle crack were loose because the winter cold had shrunk the metal. Stevie kept pulling them out and dropping them beside me. I had long since given up the luxury of being frightened. So when he fell off, I merely observed his body fly past until it was jerked to a halt by the belay. It was his pitch, and therefore it was his problem.

My problem was the Quartz Crack, where a minor storm was in progress, the sky turning black with spindrift avalanches. Stevie was left choking at the bottom of the pitch while I was saved from a long fall by the shovel of my axe jamming itself like a nut into a crack. Under the rush of the avalanche, I dangled from the axe and wondered if the maelstrom had swept Stevie away yet.

The most strung-out leads were the snow-covered Exit Chimneys. There was not a smear of ice under that teasing snow that led us on with promises of easy climbing. The underlying rock was downward-pointing, like the slates on the roofs of our houses, the ones we were too busy training to fix. The belays would not have taken a fall. There were few runners. And we had to trust and believe in each other's ability to climb to keep us both alive.

The bivouac that night was on the summit ridge; we were so cold and run-down that we couldn't sleep, hugging each other for warmth and making brews of weak tea. There was a steady but strong wind all night. We couldn't see our predicament until dawn arrived, revealing a sea of cloud below us. That was when we knew we were going to live.

It took us four hours to glissade down the west flank. This technique is not recommended. I shan't describe it here, except to say that you have to be very careful of the icy bits. It's a long way down. At the bottom of the west face the snow was so deep and soft that Stevie disappeared under the crest of a snow wave and reappeared on the other side.

We must have smelt quite a bit because skiers at the cafe moved to distant tables when we sat down. One old man did not move away, and as Stevie carefully put his mug down in the middle of the saucer, the old man leant forward and said:

'It's okay, you can relax now. That mug is not going to fall down the mountain.'

I regret not asking the old man his name. He knew. He had been there too. The tension receded. There was the overdue shower, the huge meal of spaghetti and tomato paste and garlic. And wine. Then, finally, our working protocol broke down. Until that point we hadn't allowed our emotions to interfere with the job in hand. We had been partners but not friends. Now all the suppressed irritations poured out. We were abrasive and abusive. I can't remember what about. We called each other some names. Two pig-headed climbers, we were on the verge of coming to blows, and I didn't care. Stevie lifted me by my collar till my feet were flailing inches from the ground, and I was so angry I still didn't care. I watched fascinated as his eyes bulged and the veins on the side of his neck swelled and wriggled like caterpillars. He was turning redder and redder. I understood I was about to come to some very real harm. Then, like a breaking wave, a change came over Stevie. He dropped me to the floor and burst into tears.

'Look what you nearly did, you fucking idiot! You nearly made me kill you.'

I don't remember what happened next. I guess I must have hugged him. Whatever it was, I'm sure the communards would have disapproved.

PEKAN

Left and above: Old photos of Aziza, our Malaysian *ama*, with her family.

Right: Aziza.

The plans for our house.

The main street.

Pekan river.

ENAM BELAS

Enjoying some time at the beach.

Above: Mick Fowler, Stephen Venables and me at the CIC hut.

Below: Climbing in Sussex in 1984.

Right: Nick Kagan, me and Simon Alston.

Bottom right: Tony Wilmot.
Photo: *Richard Haszko*

TRAVELS ON THE *NORTHERN FROST*

Right: My friend Ali.

Bottom: Boston harbour.

LONDON

Above: Inspirational architecture in the form of Christ Church, Spitalfields, designed by Nicholas Hawksmoor.

Right: Climbing *Magician* on the canal walls.

Below: Stephen Venables (left) and me (right) climbing at Hornsey Viaduct.

THE EIGER, WINTER 1978-79

Above: The Ramp.

Left: Me on the Traverse of the Gods.

Below: The Spider.

CLIMBING IN SCOTLAND WITH MICK FOWLER

Above: Me and Mick after *Fly Direct,*
Creagh Meagaidh.

Below: Mick attempting *Minus Buttress*, 1980.

Right: Me on *Pointless* on Ben Nevis.

Phil Thornhill on *Reasons to be Fearful*.

6

REASONS TO BE FEARFUL

(1979)

Winter 1979. The 'Winter of Discontent', as newspapers now call it. I was sitting in The Globe, a gloomy Islington pub, which was then the midweek home of the North London Mountaineering Club. It smelt of cigarettes and spilt beer. With its old oak furniture and feeble lighting, you couldn't see the floor well enough to judge what was making it so sticky – the beer, presumably. I had just returned from the Eiger. Stevie had left London for North Wales. Nick had immigrated to New Zealand. The cold, snowy winter continued, and I was looking for climbing partners.

Peering through the murk, I noticed a tousle-haired young man leaning on the bar. He appeared to be in his early twenties. The barmaid, Charlene, was leaning across the bar towards him.

'What?' she said.

'Pint of your cheapest bitter.' The young man turned to me, smiling at his own humour. 'Cheapest is always best, you know!' Then he tapped the side of his nose.

Several people had warned me about climbing anything serious with Mick Fowler. They would say: 'He only likes disgustingly loose rock. I wouldn't go anywhere with him if I were you.'

Perhaps I was already a bit drunk. Maybe it was a moment of Reverse Tourette's, when instead of blurting out inappropriate expletives, one enthuses inappropriate agreeableness. So, when Mick said he had lost his climbing partner for the following week on Ben Nevis and could I replace him, I should have said: 'No fucking way!' But what came out of my faithless mouth was, 'Yes, of course, where shall we meet?'

That weekend we drove up in Mick's battered minivan, sleeping in the back to get an early start. Somehow Mick had managed to book us into the CIC hut, a rare experience for Londoners. As things turned out, we had an excellent week but with a worrying start. It began in appalling weather so we took the opportunity to climb the relatively easy Tower Ridge in a storm. Predictably we got lost on the way down, navigating round the mountain at half height. But the snowstorm had encrusted the mountain's mythical Orion Face, so next day we set out to climb *Orion Direct*, a winter version of *The Long Climb*. Except we had no idea where it went.

'It's just like the Alps; you go up there, and there … it's all the same,' Mick said.

It wasn't and we didn't and it wasn't all the same *at all*. We ended up on something hard, *Astral Highway*, a more direct version of *Orion*. Soon I was starting up a steep pitch, which turned out to be the crux. It was a leaning right-angled corner, about twenty metres high. I didn't think I could get up without falling out of it, so I lowered off a large hexagonal nut I'd wedged into an icy groove. I couldn't find much of a belay below the nut. I banged in a quarter of a Lost Arrow piton, and the tip of a Snarg drive-in ice screw, knowing that the anchors wouldn't hold the slightest fall.

The wind got up again and wisps of snow blew across the face, stinging my eyes. I was cold and felt intimidated by the steep icy corner above me.

Mick came up and led through. I watched anxiously. He bridged across the corner, crampons scraping on the rocks as he looked for lumps of ice to settle on. There was no protection for most of this section but somehow he exuded an air of calm competence. At the top of the corner was a ledge like a crow's nest. Mick crawled on to the ledge and found a vertical crack where he could place two thin blades. The weather was now deteriorating badly and as the wind howled across the Orion Face it was triggering spindrift avalanches.

One of these waves of snow now flowed over Mick. He leant back to keep his face out of it. As he did so, the pegs popped out, one after the other. Looking up anxiously to see how things were going, I saw Mick falling towards me. I can still remember the noise. Above the hiss of spindrift was a jangling sound, the sound of ironware banging against the sidewalls of the corner and against itself: ice screws, rock pegs, nuts, axes and crampons. It seemed deafening. Mick's body struck me on its way past. I knew the belay was too weak to hold his fall, not a long one like this. I was dead. I knew it.

And then came silence.

So. This is what death is like. Painless. Quiet.

The spindrift slowly began coating my face. Calm gave way to cold. I began to shiver. Then the calm quiet of my thoughts was rudely interrupted.

'Vic? VIC!'

That's odd. Sounds like Mick. Is he here too? Are we both ... ?

'Vic ... are you okay?'

I looked up at my peg and ice screw. They were still there. The belay had not been loaded. The hex I had placed in the icy crack above had settled, shattering the ice around it and wedging itself firmly, saving both our lives. It was a small miracle. And yes, here we were together, but in this world, not the next. As if to confirm this, my left side suddenly felt bruised and sore.

'Mick, are *you* okay?'

'Yes ... but ... '

I braced myself. Bad news often began with a 'but'.

' ... but I can't find my helmet and glasses.'

I looked down. Mick had apparently landed on a bed-sized patch of snow. Just above him was a deep hole.

'Have you looked into the hole above you?'

Mick scrambled up and reached inside. There at the bottom was his helmet with glasses attached.

He had fallen forty metres, having been roughly twenty metres above me, and now being twenty below. We later reconstructed what had happened. Mick had seen the small snow patch below us and prepared himself to self-arrest on it with his axes. The main flaw in this plan was that Mick was falling upside down when he brushed past me. Instead he must have hit the end of the ropes at the same time as landing head first in the snow patch. He bounced out of the hole as the stretched rope recoiled, leaving his helmet at the bottom.

I was expecting to abseil down, but Mick had not the slightest inclination to give up now. He swarmed up the pitch again, and made sure this time that his belay pegs were hammered in up to the eye. I saw that this man was not short on determination. In time, I would resolve to become more like him. That was one of the fall's two long-lasting effects. The other was a kind of climber's superstition: from that pitch on Mick and I swapped pitches religiously. I sort of suspected that my cowardice, in handing over the lead of the crux pitch, had prompted fate to precipitate Mick's fall.

The weather next day was better, the best day of the week. We set about Mick's main project: *Shield Direct*. Because of the new Astral Highway Superstition, the first, third, fifth and seventh pitches were mine to lead. This superstition became a strict climbing rule for me. If at the end of one weekend Mick had led the last pitch, the first pitch the next day or next weekend would have to be mine. The superstition did not allow for excuses, hangovers or weekend weaknesses. And when we climbed in Russia and Pakistan on bigger mountains, like Ushba and Spantik, we kept to the same rule.

The Globe didn't only generate winter climbing. There were summers to deal with too. During the early years of Mrs Thatcher's government, my friend Phil lived in a squat. There were still squatters in those days.

Even as the government waged war on those self-same squats, he habitually voted Conservative. I worked as an architect, and had moved from Stockwell to a nice middle-class part of Islington and voted Labour. Our political lives were not much troubled by vested interests. What did trouble us though, was the discovery by Phil, Mick and others in the London climbing scene that when conditions up north in Scotland were unsatisfactory, crampons and axes could still be useful down south.

First came the soft chalk of Dover; next was the somewhat firmer stuff of Beachy Head, outside the East Sussex town of Eastbourne. And then Phil discovered that the sandstone cliffs bordering nearby Hastings were so fragile and loose that it was safer to climb using crampons and axes than rock shoes. Safer again would have been to avoid them altogether, but that did not occur to us in those days.

Phil began his campaign on these vile cliffs in the summer of 1983. Face climbing was out of the question: small ledges would peel away and there was no possibility of banging in pegs. So Phil made ascents up deep chimneys and cracks. The climbs were dirty, clogged with sea kale and sprinkled with seagull shit. Usually he climbed solo, occasionally dragging me along. We always came home gull-shit filthy and frequently in tatters from the gorse and thorn bushes that guarded the tops of the climbs. But these cracks were the only features that allowed a bit of protection. Oversize hexes, and sometimes wood or iron bars diagonally braced across the fissures, offered some slight hope of avoiding a ground fall.

That summer Phil created a collection of routes with oddly descriptive names: the *Green Ghastly*, *One in the Eye for Harold* and so on. I climbed one or two of these with Phil, but my mind has protected me since by deleting nearly all recollection of them. Age-related memory loss has its uses.

There was a reason that Phil usually climbed alone – or, as he called it, with 'RS': his silent partner Mr Rope-Solo, also known as Phil's rucksack. That reason was Phil's dreadful slowness. He climbed so slowly that many people simply refused to climb with him. But the more he soloed, the slower he became; and the slower he became, the fewer people could bear the tedium of belaying him. It was a vicious circle. On one Hastings route, the *Green Ghastly*, probably, he took five hours to climb a twenty-five-metre pitch. And as I belayed him, climbing at the heady rate of five metres an hour, I came very close to losing the will to live.

Somewhere in all the grime and birdshit of these ascents, interspersed with protective mind-emptying sessions drinking beer in The Globe, Phil came to a realisation.

'You know how the bottom and tops of the routes are bald sandstone?'

'Slurp,' the beer said.

'And there's that band of steep clay between them?'

'Slurp.'

'Well, the band of clay extends across the entire cliff. It's about a mile long. There could be a new route there.'

'Eurch!' the beer complained, as it went down the wrong opening and left me in a coughing fit.

What I meant to say was: 'Are you fucking mad?'

What actually came out of my mouth was: 'Great! When do we start?'

That damned Reverse Tourette's again.

And so, one rainy Saturday in November 1983, we began. Our starting point was the nature reserve of Ecclesbourne Glen, an evil re-entrant a mile from Hastings. From there, we climbed in the general direction of The Dolphin, the nearest pub to the beach. The climbing was, on average, about Scottish grade IV. The clay band widened and narrowed. Where it narrowed a lot, we were forced on to the frightening and unprotectable sandstone that sandwiched the clay. A hundred feet from safety in either direction, up or down, the band extended laterally for a mile. After rain, the moist clay took axe strokes and crampons pretty well: sometimes too well. Crampons would ball up with slippery clods. We found the dry clay was even more disturbing, being fragile and tending to crumble under our feet with alarming suddenness. On that first day, we did five pitches, placed two warthog ice pegs and rapped down to the beach as it got dark.

Leaving our ropes in place, we strolled the mile-long pebble beach to The Dolphin, where we slurped our beer while shedding sand, clay and dirt on their nice clean carpet. With the beer were salt-and-vinegar crisps. I pulled out a book.

'What you reading?' Phil asked, now shedding crisp crumbs on the carpet.

'*Heart of Darkness.*'

'One of the greatest novels in the English language,' he said, as though this was incontrovertible fact. I didn't know about that. I hadn't read all the others. Meanwhile, the jukebox was blaring Ian Dury numbers: 'Billericay Dickie' and then 'Reasons to be Cheerful'.

'What do you think about that for a route name?' I asked him.

'*Heart of Darkness?*'

'No. I mean the music: *Reasons to be Cheerful.*'

'I think something like *Reasons to be Fearful* would be more accurate.' So that's what we called it.

We slept in my car and on Sunday morning jugged up the ropes and managed another five pitches before deciding it was time to get back to London before the pubs closed. Leaving two warthogs and lots of bright red tape behind, we pulled our ropes down. Each visit would see one of us walking along the beach at low tide, and the other (we took turns) struggling through gorse at the top with the ropes. The beach walker's job was to spot the red tape and then tell the other where to rap down. Stringing together as many gorse bushes as possible for the anchor, the top man rapped down to the warthogs. The beach walker would then jumar up to start the day. Over the next three months we spent a total of six days on the route. On most of them, we managed between five and ten pitches. On one of them, we only climbed two.

It was Sunday. The night before, we had drunk too much beer in The Dolphin and were feeling queasy. It was my lead. I tiptoed round a buttress of disgusting clay, crampons sending dry sods gently towards the retreating tide, axes spiking steep dry soil and ripping through slightly with each placement. Phil was behind the buttress, hidden from view. So when the rope tightened, as it does at the end of a pitch, pulling me slightly off balance, I placed the usual belay of two warthogs and waited for the rope to slacken, signalling that Phil had started to follow.

This being Phil, it didn't surprise me much that nothing happened for a while. Also, I felt unwell from the night before. I suppose at this point I must have fallen asleep, because when I opened my eyes, the sun had moved towards the horizon. I pulled the rope hard and shouted for Phil to get going. The rope snagged a bit and then, with a shower of gravel, it pulled through freely. In fact, a lot of rope pulled through, about half of it. I realised I had not been at the end of the pitch at all, just at the end of a jammed rope. Phil, used to his own slow pace, had taken advantage of the rope jam to snooze, unseen by me, on his side of the buttress. We had both of us slept for over two hours. When Phil arrived at my stance, we rapped off for the week.

Far across the beach, under the long cliff, a small dust cloud appeared in the wake of a posse. As it drew closer, we could see police helmets and some kind of coastguard uniform leading the group. They looked intimidating.

'Intriguing,' said Phil.

'What's happening?' I asked the first to arrive.

'Well,' said the constable, 'we're on a rescue mission.'

'Oh really?'

'Yes, we've just had a report that two men are stuck fast on the cliff near here. Have you seen them?'

'Oh no, officer,' I said, shielding my dirty rucksack from his line of sight.

'Nope,' said Phil. 'Not seen anything unusual at all.'

'You might not have noticed them. They were unconscious.'

'I'm pretty sure they're not round here,' I said. 'Perhaps you should try the very far end of the cliff; we haven't been down there.'

'Right! To the far end!' said the constable, and sticking out his chin he marched off, determined to complete his mission, the officious posse behind him casting the odd backward glance at us.

Phil asked why I had sent the rescue party to the far end of the cliffs.

'To give us maximum time to get away before they figure it out. And we'd better give it a couple of weeks before we come back.' I really didn't want to inconvenience the law enforcement of Hastings, but it was nearly opening time. As a result of the quite reasonable fear of being rumbled, we didn't complete the route until January 1984.

In the summer of that year, the North London Mountaineering Club mounted an expedition to Hunza in Pakistan's Karakoram range. The team was made up of the usual Scottish- and chalk-climbing weekenders. We didn't get up our mountain. With Phil, I endured a fourteen-day climb with six days' food. Chris dropped his boot from 6,000 metres and Mick tried to boil his own helmet. To cap it all, he also insisted that if we ever made it back to London, he and I should have a boxing match.

7

SECONDS OUT

(1986)

The whole boxing thing began in a tent on the Hunza expedition. Tents are interesting: they insulate you from space and time. From the outside, a tent is a small insignificant dot in the landscape. From the inside, it is the whole universe. Following the theory of the (purported) 'lost child' Kaspar Hauser, tents, like the dungeon he was raised in, are larger than the outside, because when outside you can see the landscape *and* the tent. But from the inside, you see only the tent, which wholly obscures the outside world, meaning the tent must be bigger.

So in this tent somewhere in Pakistan, which was hidden from view, Mick Fowler began to talk about London. For all we knew, we could have been there: in London, in the tent, camped on the pavement, drinkers staggering past us on the way from the pub to the Indian restaurant. I felt the tent rustle; maybe it was a glacial breeze, maybe a drunk passing too close to our section of pavement. Mick rolled on to his side and said:

'I know a pub where you can box your friends.'

'You mean a gym?'

'No, I mean a pub. Where you can box your friends. There's a ring and a referee and they have gloves you can borrow.'

'Okay, next weekend.'

There it was: the start of something new. Suddenly I had questions.

'But, fighting? I don't know how to do that.'

'Easy, just like in school.'

I didn't say anything, but I didn't think I had been to the same kind of school as Mick.

'But, what about wearing glasses?'

'Easy, just put in your contact lenses.'

We must have been at the end of the expedition, or else we were already in London. In any case, next weekend came, and so did we, to the Kings in Seven Kings, not a pub but a nightclub in Ilford. I drove over from Islington with the young alpinist Andy Fanshawe, who had agreed to be my second. The saloon bar was long, and at its far end was a boxing ring. The atmosphere was boozy, filled with tobacco smoke and a sort of blood lust. A man in a check suit was telling jokes over the PA. He was in the middle of a story about a prostitute and a lorry driver.

Mick and his second, Simon Fenwick, eventually found us. The place was heaving. Judging by the tattoos on display, the Kings served as watering hole to the local branch of the National Front, a forerunner of the far-right British National Party, with strong views on race. I hadn't become any more fair-skinned than I had been at school, and after a few weeks climbing in glaciated mountains I had gone very dark indeed. Without a shirt on, it was obvious from my untanned body that I was European. But my face had taken on the shades of Asia. And here we were, fresh back from Pakistan. Perhaps I shouldn't have mentioned that so often when asked. I was already getting some strange looks from the other customers.

The Kings was in Fenwick's backyard, so he explained it all to me when we arrived.

'They have a pub professional here.'

'Eh?'

'The boxing ring: you can fight your friend or you can fight the pub professional.'

'Hmm.'

'They had Nigel Benn here once.'

'But this is skinhead territory?'

'Yeah, but it was Nigel Benn. They don't mind blacks if they can box.'

'Oh, I see. A bit like tenpin bowling, I suppose.' I had a happy image of a huge black ball scattering white skittles.

'Eh?' Fenwick was shaking his head. He couldn't grasp what I was saying against the noise. He shouted: 'It's Asians they don't like.'

'Oh.'

Glasses and the fight game do not go together. I had learnt that in the tent. So the day before our bout, I found an optician who sold me some contact lenses. I had forgotten to ask how to use them but now set off to the loo to try and figure that out.

The face in the mirror grimaced at me as I tried to poke contact lenses into his eyes. Yet the only contact the lenses seemed to make was with his fingers and cheeks. Like identical poles, the lenses seemed magnetically repulsed from the corneas. After half an hour I gave up and emerged from the loo with red eyes, my vision blurred, having failed quite comprehensively to insert the lenses. I was just going to have to try without. I dropped my spectacles in the sink for safekeeping and returned to the bar. Pushing through the crowd without them would be good training for the fight, I thought. Provided I didn't spill anyone's beer.

The man in the check suit was now telling a story about a Pakistani and a lorry driver. He seemed quite keen on lorry drivers. He had a hoarse, smoke-damaged voice and a loud tie that only emphasised his rolls of neck fat. He was enjoying himself, and the audience chuckled beerily at his coarse jokes.

Without my glasses, I couldn't see him clearly. I couldn't see anything clearly. It was all a blur, a bit like opening your eyes underwater in a pool. At the edge of my vision I could make out the one black man in the room. He was huge, and no one was bothering him. I managed to make my way over without bumping into anyone.

'Hello.'

He turned round slowly. 'Yes?'

'I've never boxed before.'

'And?'

'I'm fighting my friend. The one over there? He's bigger than me. I don't know your name, but I wonder if you could possibly help me. Any tips on how to survive, for instance?'

'S'easy. You just hold your mitts up – like this. He jabs at you – you keep your guard up, duck and weave. Kna-wha'-I-mean?'

Ignoring the shake of my head, he put his fists either side of his temples. Peeping through the gap he said: 'You have to move, use your legs.' The professional danced around a bit to illustrate the point. 'And when there's a gap in his guard, you smack him – like this.'

He jabbed his left, stopping an inch from my nose. It was actually rather a beautiful movement. Starting from his right toe, you could see the force flowing through his body to culminate in the weapon that was his fist. Then he shook my hand for luck and pushed me in the general direction of the ring.

Our seconds, Fenwick and Fanshawe, helped us lace up the big red boxing mitts. Then we climbed into the ring and touched fists. The ref introduced us to the crowd, who began to howl and bay. He said various things, which I couldn't hear. I noticed how much harder it is to hear without spectacles, but this didn't seem like the right moment to reflect on that. I expect the referee was explaining the rules he wanted us to fight by. I was still trying to listen, head cocked to one side, boxing mitt to my ear like some kind of ear trumpet, when he stood aside.

The bell rang and I immediately understood the disadvantage of not being able to see. From out of the blur emerged a charging Fowler. There was a sort of aura, a halo around him, which on closer inspection resolved itself into a cloud of whirling arms and fists. I think this might be called the 'windmill technique', but I'm not sure. The crowd of faces round the ring cheered and roared.

I don't remember the pain so much as the noise – noise and a very confused state of mind. I had the recommended guard up to each side of my head. I could more or less squint through the gap between my gloves. I was doing everything right and still the blows were raining down all round my head. While it was true that Mick was not battering my face, now guarded, he was hammering the top of my head, my neck, my shoulders, and even the back of my head. How did he reach there?

The pub professional had not given me any advice about countering windmills, so I retreated gracefully. That is to say, I ran away into the ropes of the ring. I had forgotten about the ropes and didn't see them till they emerged from the blur of faces at chest height. The Fowler fists were now drumming on my back. The crowd was going wild. The bout had only just started and already they were howling. I thought I might be in danger from them too.

They were chanting, all together: 'Kill 'im! Kill 'im! Kill 'im!'

Kill him? It takes a while to understand you are the object of universal hatred. Plus, I was somewhat preoccupied. Even so, the realisation did finally dawn on me that the crowd wanted me dead. They wanted my opponent to kill me. Me. Not all of us are swift at taking hostility to heart, but it did seem rather personal, and such thoughts do not offer peace of mind to the *ingénu* boxer. I held my gloves up against the onslaught. I weaved. I ducked, usually straight into an oncoming fist. I still don't fully understand how that's supposed to work.

Throughout the bout, the referee remained a white blur with a dark patch marking out his natty bow tie. I am not particularly anti-authoritarian. I don't make a habit of blaming umpires, but in this case I have to say the referee was not much help. Every time I got behind him, he moved out of the way. He just would not stay put. And every time he stepped aside, there was Mick and the crowd cheering him on.

'Go-fer-it! Kill 'im! Kill 'im! KILL 'IM!'

I had been told the bout would last a minute, but it was a very long sixty seconds. More like an hour, I would have said. I have often wondered if the ref kept it going to entertain the crowd. As time passed, the Fowler windmill slowed down a little; at times he seemed to be resting his tired hands on me. I understood Mick had finally exhausted himself when he collapsed on to my shoulders in a kind of tired bear hug. The referee stepped in to separate us.

At this point, I remembered the words of the pub professional and attempted a right jab in the general direction of Mick's face. But I think I may have caught the referee because immediately he sat down. When he got up again, he kicked me in the shin and, to uproar from the disappointed crowds, stopped the fight.

Back in the loo, someone had removed my glasses from the basin. Punch-drunk and half blind, I staggered back to the bar, pushing through the crowd, who had now forgotten me. Fenwick and Fowler had lined up several pints for me.

'Great entertainment!' Fenwick said, slapping me on the back and handing over my spectacles. 'I rescued these from the bog.'

I had a headache for days. At work someone asked me who had won.

'I can't say,' I said, and then thought awhile. 'But I don't think it was me.'

8

K2

(1993)

Under a faultless blue sky at Urdukas, Razzaq (later dubbed the 'Baltoro Blackadder') was watching a grass snake writhing under a thorn bush. This is the last place on the way to K2 where you can find bushes, grass and flowers, and distressed reptiles. Beyond Urdukas, all is sterile glacier, moraine heaped like spoil-tips and ice-sheathed mountains. One of the German climbers setting up a tent next to me said:

'She is not so well, this *Schlange*.'

'If you were English, I would know you are a zoologist.'

'Why?'

'We have no gender for animals in English. Only a specialist would know this one is female. Very hard to see its privates from here.'

And that got me pondering. While German has three genders, French two and English one (or is it none?), just across the Baltoro watershed, in the Hunza valley, they have four genders. Why? Why and how would multiple genders help in a language? Could you use genders to improve the efficiency of language? For example, in French the word *poêle* changes meaning with gender. *Le poêle* is a stove, while *la poêle* is a frying pan. *La tour* is a tower, *le tour* a turn. And so on.

German could theoretically save even more words: *der Band* is a volume or set of books; *das Band* is a ribbon; and *die Band*, well, that plays music. Standing in my mental oasis, I became lost in thought:

In French, with fifty words plus the two gender words, fifty-two words in total, you could name a hundred different things while in English we would need a hundred words.

In German, you could have thirty-three nouns plus three gender words, a total of thirty-six words to describe the same number of objects. More efficient. In Burushaski, the language of the Hunza valley, it would be twenty-five plus four, making twenty-nine.

What would be the most efficient number of genders? Let's say we have a language of one hundred objects. Well, with ten noun words and ten gender words (the square root rule) you could describe everything. But what of the cube root? If you had gender words for genders? You could have four gender-gender words, five gender words and five nouns. A total of fourteen words for a hundred different things. The fourth root gives diminishing returns with thirteen in total if you have four noun words, three gender words, three gender-gender words, and three gender-gender-gender words, allowing a hundred and eight objects to be named. While the fifth root ...

Then I became aware that my new German friend was peering into my face with apparent concern, having turned his attention away from the *Schlange*.

'Are you also not well?'

'What? I mean, why?'

'It is because,' he said slowly, 'you stopped talking and a strange look has come over your face, like sick or drunk.'

'Ah. Sorry. Actually, I was thinking.' But I didn't explain what I was thinking. It would only confirm to them that in fact I was *not* well, not well at all.

Three days later we were all camped under K2, and a week or two after settling in, we held the 'Godwin-Austen Games'. I cannot remember whose idea it was, but probably the two Germans: Reinmar Joswig and Peter Metzger. They were always organising things. The Swedish team wore Viking helmets, with horns. There was a competition to throw either ice axes or boots. There was something to do with potato sacks and hopping. Teams had a poem to read and a song to sing. My photographs show participants whiling away a rest day, prompted most likely by a spell of poor weather. The atmosphere in these images is social, contented. There is no hint of the tragedy that would unfold in the coming days.

There were seven other expedition teams on the Godwin-Austen glacier that year. They had assembled somewhat haphazardly over the preceding days and weeks, along a whaleback moraine of red-brown rocks strewn over the glacier and dubbed the Strip.

The Strip was a pop-up township: a string of canvas hamlets. Each expedition grouped their tents around their dining marquee. On one side of the strip, there was a shallow depression in the ice, along which, in the daytime, in good weather, a surface stream flowed and was used as the water supply. The higher the expedition camp, the cleaner the water.

There were around seventy people on the Strip that summer. It was difficult to be exact. It was a truly international community. In alphabetical order, for want of a more logical system, climbers came from America, Australia, Austria, Britain, Canada, Croatia, Denmark, Germany, Holland, Mexico, New Zealand, Pakistan (of course), Russia, Slovenia, Spain, Sweden and probably several other countries I cannot recall. All four hemispheres were represented, though the north and the west predominated. Most people on the Strip spoke English as a second or third language. Most people on the Strip were men. Most people would be on the Strip for two months, some a little longer, a few somewhat less.

Above the Strip, the south face of K2 rose in a squat pyramid for 3,500 metres. The top third consisted of red rocks apparently floating on rounded snow ridges that looked as innocuous as rolling white fields.

I almost expected to see green sheep grazing under the sun. When the sun did shine, and the sky was free of cloud, there were only three colours: paper-white snow, rust-red rock and the indigo sky.

The south face of K2 looks down directly on the Strip. The right-hand skyline forms the 'normal' route, the Abruzzi spur, the line of the first ascent in 1954. On the mountain's left horizon, a ridge emerges and rises to a rocky prominence called the Point Negrotto. It then descends in a series of red pinnacles to the glacier. It is on the last and lowest of these that the Gilkey Memorial stands. A dusty path leads up from the tortured glacier under the last pinnacle, but the final few feet are a cantilevered stone pavement, typical of this part of Pakistan. This place has for many decades been a shrine to the dead.

Everywhere I looked, there were hammered aluminium plates, one decked with dry flowers and inscribed in neat Japanese Kanji, another in Polish. By 1993 there had been around eighty ascents of K2, and around thirty fatalities. And each death had been commemorated here with a plaque, following the example of Mario Puchoz's memorial from 1954. Most of these plaques were aluminium expedition plates, crudely hammered to show the name and a heartbroken message to the dead. A yard further and there was a mound of these plates draped over the cairn. Tibetan prayer flags fluttered their mantras on the wind.

The first deaths on K2 were in 1939, and here there was a sad coincidence because one plate read: 'In memory of Julie Tullis 1939–1986'. Al Rouse, who also perished in 1986, was commemorated by a plate so badly rusted it could barely be read at all. Behind the cairn, the great and wide ice rivers of the Godwin-Austen, the Savoia, and the Vigne and Baltoro glaciers merged in a majestic sweep at Concordia. Above the gentle curves of the glaciers, Marble Peak, Crystal Peak, Mitre Peak and the massive Broad Peak took guard. Enigmatic Chogolisa looked on from a distance.

The Gilkey Memorial felt like an altar, Chogolisa the western towers of a cathedral, and the Godwin-Austen glacier the pilgrim's way by which you approach. As a climber, when you come to K2, you carry two rucksacks. One is full of equipment. The other, the weightier rucksack, is full of history.

There have been many expeditions to K2 since 1954 and the first ascent. Most of the ridges have been climbed. The mountain has seen ascents in every possible style, from Benoît Chamoux's solo ascent in twenty-three hours, done in the glare of publicity, to the more private and controversial attempt by Tomo Česen. Our expedition was meant to climb the Abruzzi, and the team was small. Our leader, Roger Payne, was a Londoner with a tousle of black hair, a huge smile and an even larger enthusiasm for life. He was married to Julie-Ann Clyma, a mountain guide and PhD from New Zealand who was stronger at altitude than most of us. Paired to climb with me was Alan Hinkes, who would later claim the title of first Englishman to climb all the 8,000-metre peaks.

In addition, we had with us an expedition doctor, Caroline Williams from Bristol; a liaison officer delegated from the Pakistani army, Captain Nayyer Abbassi, who extended his job description to provide us with moral support; and finally, our cook Razzaq, who Roger called the Baltoro Blackadder on account of his sense of humour, although his dress sense was closer to that of Baldrick.

Since the Strip was home to eccentrics and obsessives, it's hardly surprising that there were outbreaks of apparent insanity. One leader discovered his expedition was technically bankrupt and couldn't afford porters to leave the Strip. He went into hiding at Camp 1 and wasn't seen again for weeks. His deputy couldn't take the strain and was seen raiding the expedition supply of Valium.

There were stories of another kind. Just before we arrived at the end of June, an 'International Slovenian' expedition put four climbers on the summit of K2 within two and a half weeks of arrival, and one more after a further two weeks. In their haste, the first group of summiteers all but repeated the tragedy of 1986, as the following extract from their expedition report suggests:

The expedition's progress was smooth until shortly before the top of the climb, when the weather worsened. [Stipe] Božić, Viki Grošelj, Carlos Carsolio and Zvonko Požgaj were only able to touch the summit, because standing on it would have been impossible due to high winds. On the way back, the team got lost in the snowstorm, but ultimately managed to get to Camp 4, where they found Boris Sedej and Boštjan Kekec. The latter was in distress, showing symptoms of hypoxia, his condition worsening. Due to the urgency of the situation, Sedej, Požgaj and Božić descended with Kekec through the snowstorm. Soon Kekec was unable to walk and became unresponsive, and the trio pulled him through the deep snow. When this became physically too difficult and when Požgaj began to suffer from frostbite, they decided to leave Kekec to die on the mountain. Božić was affected by snow blindness and barely made it to safety, using only the climbing rope to direct himself back to the base camp.

When the survivors eventually reached base camp, Carlos told us his slightly different version of the story. He and Viki had lost their way on the descent from the summit and were forced to bivouac out in the open before finding the tiny two-man tent at Camp 4. In this version, the entire team was forced to wait out the storm for their third night in this tiny two-man tent. By now Carsolio had a frostbitten foot and climbed very slowly down to Camp 3 with Viki Grošelj, with whom he soon lost touch. Carlos must have nerves of steel. After he became separated from Viki, which seems to have been a habit on this climb, he spent the next thirteen hours hopelessly lost in the wind and snow, climbing up and down, looking for an elusive clue to which direction he should take.

'Een one moment I could not see anytheeng,' he told us. 'But I felt a crevasse. And een that moment I made the hard deceesion to jump. You know?'

He could not have known how far he had to jump or what was waiting for him across the white hole: horizontal ground or vertical drop; void or ledge; life or death. It is not unusual for members of an expedition to give contradictory histories of a taxing climb. The hypoxia and exhaustion tend to veil the memory. This is normal.

K2 was not the first close call for Carlos. In 1987 he was descending from Makalu when he became suddenly very ill. He probably had HAPE.[3] Two Polish climbers ignored his pleas for help. They were on their way to the summit. He had given up hope for himself and had radioed his farewells to his wife when a Catalan team lead by Josep 'Pepe' Aced picked him up, and with the later help of Alan Hinkes – sharing mountains with Carlos again – brought him safely from the mountain. One of the two Polish climbers failed to return from the summit. A week after we arrived at K2, Pepe Aced turned up with a large team of Catalans. For a few days, Carlos, Alan and Pepe were sharing the same patch of glacier again. Alan Hinkes was pleased to see Carlos, with whom he had climbed Shishapangma.

Of the six who set out from Camp 4 on 13 June, Kekec did not survive, while Požgaj and Carlos escaped with serious frostbite. It was a wake-up call. The statistics were not good, but worse was to follow.

On 7 July, a month after the Slovenians had first reached the summit, it was the turn of the Canadian–American team of Dan Culver, Jim Haberl and Phil Powers. Culver and Haberl set off at 2.30 a.m. from Camp 4, Powers forty-five minutes later. Two more Americans, Stacy Allison and John Petroske, hoped to try the next day. Haberl travelled light with no rucksack; Culver took spare clothes, two cameras, spare lenses and summit flags. It was a full moon, and they did not need headlamps. Above them loomed the huge sérac that was to kill so many climbers in 2008. Haberl later wrote that he counted fifteen breaths for each step. At that rate, they were going to spend many, many hours under those ice cliffs. By 4 a.m. Phil Powers had caught up with the pair, and forged ahead, breaking trail up to the feature known as the Bottleneck, the shallow gully that leads up to the sérac barrier.

---

3   high-altitude pulmonary (o)edema.

Powers reached the summit at 3 p.m. On his way down, he met Haberl and then Culver, who had jettisoned his rucksack above the Bottleneck. They were an hour or two behind Powers, and started down at 5 p.m. with just an hour of daylight left. It must have been dusk when they reached the Bottleneck. Back at base camp, Haberl told us he had seen Culver's ice axe placed upright in the snow. It might be that in filming Haberl's descent he lost the visual clues necessary for balance and toppled forward into the abyss, leaving his axe where he had planted it.

Later Haberl wrote that he had heard a loud sound and then saw Culver's purple and yellow down suit tumble wildly past him, funnelling down the Bottleneck, picking up speed and disappearing over mixed ground and bluffs above the south face before cartwheeling out of sight. Haberl screamed for help, then followed Culver's impact trail for 250 metres. He found his beanie and tracks left by his body, but the traces ended at a cliff edge. Haberl sat down and cried. Allison and Petroske and John Haigh, meanwhile, had climbed up to Haberl and they all returned to Camp 4.

The weather was now deteriorating fast and by 3 a.m. a full-on storm hit the tent. Haberl had fitful nightmares of a broken Culver crawling back to the tent while the others braced the tent fabric against the storm. They all left camp at 6 a.m. in a maelstrom, picking their way down by marker wands they had placed on the way up.

Arriving at Camp 2 in the early afternoon, Haberl was too exhausted to continue and stayed another night at 6,800 metres with Petroske, descending to base next day. In the continuing storm their troubles were not yet over. Avalanched and half buried, all Haberl could say to Petroske was, 'Let's go home, John!' Culver's body was never recovered. A few weeks later a memorial service was held for him at Mount Seymour United Church in North Vancouver. Haberl perished in an avalanche while skiing in to an Alaskan mountain some six years later.

By 30 July, our small team had established a dump of gas and food in a snow cave at Camp 3 at 7,400 metres. The next day, Julie-Ann and Roger enlarged the cave, while Alan and I pushed on, with the idea of leaving a tent at Camp 4 at 8,000 metres. The weather was fine, and six climbers had stood on the summit the day before. The two Germans, Reinmar and Peter, Andrew Lock from Australia and the Russian–Kazakh Anatoli Boukreev were in one team. Daniel Bidner from Sweden and Rafael Jensen from Denmark were in another.

After breaking trail for three hours from the snow cave at Camp 3, I was at 7,800 metres. The sky was clear. A light breeze was blowing wisps of snow from the ridges and buttresses above us. The valley below was filled with whirlpool clouds. A muffled shout floated up to me from Alan Hinkes, who was calling through his balaclava:

'There they are!'

I sank to my knees, wheezing a little as asthmatics will insist on doing. On the horizon, small figures staggered into view: one, two and later a third. No more.

'Where are the others now?' I wondered. Six climbers had reached the summit the day before, but even as our eyes searched the ragged horizon for further signs of life, our ears could already hear the distant tolling of church bells.

From Camp 4, an icy slope leads up to the shallow gully of the Bottleneck, which, after fifty metres, is followed by a traverse out to the left under the sérac barrier. This gives access to upper snow slopes that lead, unrelentingly, to the summit at 8,611 metres. The six climbers had left their tents at 4 a.m. and reached the top between 4.30 p.m. and 8 p.m. Rafael radioed his base from the summit to say he was standing there with Andrew Lock. Unfortunately, Rafael thought Lock's name was Cook. His base thought he said he was there with his 'cook from Switzerland' and assumed he was suffering from cerebral oedema. Andrew and Anatoli reached their tent by dusk. Rafael waited at the traverse for the others, who were soon overtaken by nightfall.

For a while, Rafael could see two head torches descending unevenly, missing the track they had made in the morning. He knew Daniel was one of them. So one of the three Germans must already be missing. In the dark, the men were slowly dying from oxygen starvation and hypothermia. Rafael shouted instructions: go left there, down a bit, too far right and so on. By now, Daniel was hallucinating. He had been married just a few weeks before leaving for this trip. In his mind, he was back in Sweden, and Camp 4 was a hut by the road. He had to reach the hut and then all would be fine. As long as his hallucinations corresponded to a need to climb down, he had a chance of survival. Sometime during that long night, the remaining German head torch disappeared. The delightful Peter and Reinmar would no longer be organising games on the ice.

Daniel reached the traverse just before dawn and Rafael helped him to the start of the bottleneck. Soon it was daybreak, but Rafael's own survival was now at risk. His toes had begun to freeze while waiting. He started climbing down to Camp 4; Daniel would have to descend the last few hundred feet to camp unaided. He never made it. Daniel was last seen rolling down the mountain, clutching something in his arms and wearing a blissful and relaxed expression on his face. For him, the struggle was over. Perhaps his hallucination had changed. The effort was almost too much for Rafael, who was found by Andrew face down in front of his tent. The Australian picked the poor, brave man up, put a sleeping bag in his rucksack and forced him down towards Camp 3. Two hours later Alan saw them approaching.

'There they are!'

I took over from Andrew, while Alan was given Rafael's sack to carry. Rafael could now barely walk; he would fall over and collapse after every three steps. During one of these collapses, while we sat looking at Broad Peak North and far below us, the Godwin-Austen glacier, Rafael said to me:

'Where are you from, Wik?'

'I live in a small village in Scotland, you won't have heard of it.'

'Which willage, Wik?'

'Alyth, tiny village, two churches and three pubs.'

'The Losset, Burnside and the Airlie Street,' Rafael said, naming all three pubs correctly. 'But the Airlie Street is called Joey's because the old man that had it before was called Joe.'

'What? I mean, what? How?'

'I used to live in Alyth.'

'What were you doing there?'

'I was working in nurseries.'

'Nurseries? Are you a teacher?'

'Tree nurseries.'

I wanted to ask more, but Rafael had fallen asleep again, dreaming that Daniel was there with him.

At Camp 3, Roger and Julie-Ann had tea ready, and an enlarged snow cave too. The next day, the two of them worked hard to bring the exhausted and frostbitten Dane down 2,000 metres to the glacier. Below Camp 3 there are old fixed ropes. Many of the ropes are worn and frayed; they can be very dangerous. Somewhere here Roger took a fall when an old rope snapped. With the right combination of snow conditions, weather and acclimatisation, the Abruzzi is reasonably straightforward. Remove any one of these preconditions and the mountain becomes lethal.

In spite of the Baltoro Blackadder's excellent cooking, our enthusiasm for the mountain was ebbing fast. Six people had stood on the summit the day Alan and I were going up to Camp 3. Only three were still alive the next day. The weather had been perfect; there was nothing other than altitude to kill them. The odds had sharpened considerably: twenty per cent, then thirty-three and now fifty per cent fatalities. Would the next group continue this upward curve? Years later I was asked if I had felt cheated of the summit by the rescue.

'No,' I responded. 'The opposite is true. The rescue probably saved my life. The next team was due to lose seventy-five per cent of the team. There were two of us. Do the maths.'

After Rafael was helicoptered out from base, there followed a three-week period of appalling weather. Blizzards swept across our tents and the snow cave at Camp 3 collapsed under the weight of eight feet of snow. For us, this signalled the end of the expedition; our two-month sojourn on the Strip was over. We were at last free to go home.

Before we left, there was a surreal and slightly unsettling incident. Art Gilkey's remains from exactly forty years earlier appeared scattered in a diagonal line across the glacier by our camp. First, we found a femur; then pieces of clothing that were 1950s American army surplus in origin; then the remains of a down jacket with Eddie Bauer buttons; a section of jaw with half a dozen teeth, from which a forensic dentist later identified his age as thirty-five to forty-five, his diet as western; and finally, to clinch it all, a supernumerary tooth in the upper jaw, which his family remembered.

We were at Camp 2 the day our porters began to arrive. The following day, we reached base sagging under huge rucksacks full of tents, down suits and climbing gear. We packed away our cluster of tents and our kitchen marquee, and boxed up Art Gilkey's remains. The following day, a period of perfectly fine, clear weather began as we toiled back down the Baltoro glacier.

At Urdokas, Razzaq, the Baltoro Blackadder, pointed at the faultless sky.

'When you find Gilkey, bad weather. Now you take Gilkey, good weather.'

I said not a word in reply. I was thinking about the ones we had left behind: Reinmar, Peter and Daniel. I was gazing at the granite spires around us: Lobsang, climbed by Doug Scott; Trango Tower, climbed by Joe Brown; Uli Biaho, climbed by John Roskelley; and a host of other peaks, all beautiful, each with their own history. And us, walking down with ours.

9

THE DARK COULOIR

(1996)

My usual experience of leaving the plane at Islamabad was like stepping into a sauna. This time, in late October, on my way to climb Nanga Parbat in winter, it was more like Edinburgh in summer, but without the rain.

I was now forty-six years old and supposedly more mature, though many of my friends would have doubted that. I'd spent the evening before my flight with Roger and Ghazala Mear, who had been on honeymoon to Nanga Parbat base camp. I reasoned that a drink with the Mears would be useful expedition research, but the third bottle of Pinot had been a mistake. I had a terrible headache and was in no mood to argue with Pakistani taxi drivers. On top of overcharging by an astronomical amount, my man decided to lecture me on Rawalpindi hotels.

'You not go to Shalimar. No good hotel. You go to Holiday Hotel.'

'But I really want to go to the Shalimar. Please take me there.'

'No. You go to Holiday. This my town. I know Rawalpindi. I tell you about hotel here. You are from Germany? When I am tourist in Germany, you tell me which hotel. Now I tell you hotel.'

It was no use arguing. We drove to the Holiday Hotel, and then after that we drove to the Shalimar, where Rafael Jensen was waiting for me.

Since our experiences on K2 three years earlier, he had visited me in Alyth, arriving from Sweden by motorbike, a twenty-year-old BMW R90S. This Rafael was not the down-suited mountaineer I remembered, but a lanky, long-haired biker who spoke with a strong accent and what I could only take to be Scandinavian sentence construction. Over drinks in the pub and bottles of red at home, we talked each other into trying to climb in the Himalaya in winter. As a team of two. With no support above base camp. Once again, the effect of alcohol had made itself felt in my life.

I booked us into a room at the Shalimar and collapsed on to the bed as the jet lag hit me. Next morning we were blessed with that most rare of all rarities, a flight from Islamabad to Gilgit. Checking in, Rafael was quite surprised, since he was in the domestic terminal, to be approached by a customs official wanting to relieve him of his supply of expedition alcohol. The official seemed happy to take the port but Rafael was allowed to keep the Lagavulin 'for medicinal purposes'. Perhaps his boss didn't like the taste of single malt. I suppose we have to be thankful for small mercies in this world.

The flight to Gilgit is nothing short of wonderful. Take it if you ever have the chance. The aircraft follows the Kaghan valley, littered with low-altitude climbing objectives, many of them untrodden. This time, the Kaghan peaks with their small alpine glaciers were blanketed with snow. Then Nanga Parbat appeared in the windows. The Diamir face began to scroll past. I took a few stereo shots while Rafael ran a couple of films through his camera. We gawped quite a bit at the obviously huge height differential between summit and glacier.

Rafael said: 'Only a small plane can fly this close. Wonderful. I love these machines, the old prop planes that run for decades. This is real air service: small machines flying to remote places like this and Baffin Island.'

Squinting at the mountain from under the wing, I couldn't help noticing strips of duct tape apparently holding the landing gear together. Our machine was a Fokker of some kind, and I half remembered that the company no longer existed. I began to wonder if there was some link between Fokker's bankruptcy and the need to improvise repairs with strips of duct tape.

Just north of Nanga was a lone 7,400-metre peak easily accessible from Gilgit: Haramosh, the last big mountain for Tony Streather, one of the survivors of the 1953 K2 expedition. The tragic cautionary tale of the Haramosh expedition was captured in *The Last Blue Mountain*, among the best mountaineering books ever written.

The pilots invited us to the cockpit to see Nanga Parbat, and asked how long we would be on the mountain. We said two months, and by the time we answered, we had flown past it. Behind us, the mountain showed her Rakhiot face. I had never seen any place look so cold; wisps of snow drifted lazily from the summit ridge over the layered séracs, chalky with fresh cold snow. There was a frosty matt effect to the whole face. Clearly it had seen no sun for some time. Waves of white 6,000-metre peaks continued to scroll past the portholes. The scenery was just amazing. But the pilots displayed a disdainful professional boredom that suggested they were just high-altitude bus drivers after all.

The Fokker shuddered horribly as it landed, and with dry mouths we staggered out into the thin air and sharp light of Gilgit. Our barrels of expedition gear were waiting for us at the hotel, but before we could leave for the mountain we had to go shopping. The bazaar at Gilgit runs along a road almost two kilometres long. There was merchandise from China and produce from the northern Pakistani districts of Hunza and Chitral, as well as goods from the big cities to the south. And in the best tradition of Central Asian bazaar towns, Gilgit had a mix of cultures and languages, though Shina remained the dominant language. The bazaar was punctuated by three roundabouts, each with traffic cops doing beautifully choreographed ballet. But the pirouetting policemen were simply ignored by the scrummage of Suzuki vans and jeeps passing through. Once we felt we had enough flour, tea, sugar, milk and kerosene to last us a month, we hired one of these vans to take us seventy-five miles to Bunar Das, our road head.

'How long will it take?' Rafael asked the driver.

'Bunar Das arriving morning nine o'clock, *inshallah!*'

Sadly, Allah was not willing.

The Karakoram Highway had collapsed at a point about twenty kilometres short of Bunar Das; it took us all day to ferry loads across the break and then hire, at extortionate cost, a second van for the remainder of the journey. We were now under the outlying slopes of Nanga, and wondered if this was just the mountain's opening salvo. The second van took us to a filling station in the middle of a bone-dry desert.

'This Bunar Das.'

Somehow, I had expected something bigger.

Arranging our twelve loads around the tent, Rafael settled down to wait for porters to arrive. I went for a walk and met a jaunty young man who introduced himself as Shakar Khan and offered to arrange all our porter needs. He spoke just enough English to communicate, which was a considerable improvement on my Urdu.

Back at the tent, Rafael's ploy had worked well. He found himself surrounded by the most villainous band of ruffians, each armed with a rifle of dubious origin and a bandolier of ammunition. There were Chinese, Pakistani and even Russian-made Kalashnikovs. There were copies of M16s, ancient BSAs and even something that looked like a Lee–Enfield from the First World War. Several of the weapons were still armed with bayonets, though these were invariably folded down or sheathed. These men were all would-be porters. One evil-looking fellow said he was called Wakil, and claimed to be the local contractor for porters. They were, he declared, 'less than donkeys', so we should not deal with them directly. We thought it might be better not to deal with Wakil and to use Shakar Khan, although it turned out later that Shakar was paying his countrymen quite a bit less than he was asking for them.

The road to Diamroi was a dusty affair that passed through ten kilometres of dry gorge and scree slopes. Originally built to take vehicles, it had fallen into disrepair during its first winter season and had never been mended. Given that canyons and landslides cut it at such regular intervals, it is difficult to conceive what possessed the government to build it in the first place. Despite it being October, the day was hot. Rafael so far forgot himself as to strip down to his waist. His rucksack weighed thirty-five kilograms, while mine was a paltry twenty-eight kilograms. However, that twenty-eight kilograms equated to forty-six per cent of my body weight, so the sack hurt, my legs felt tired and I was thirsty.

'I will have to reduce the load a bit tomorrow,' I muttered to myself. 'I am less than a donkey.'

A thin traffic of bullocks, goats and small family groups passed either way. The first of these family groups included four women who took one look at Rafael, a bare-chested Viking, and hid until he had passed. No one here greets a fully clothed non-family member of the opposite sex, far less one not wearing a shirt.

The road climbed high above the valley and, though there was a torrent below, all above was desert. Stones kicked from the path sent plumes of dust into the air as they tumbled down the scree slopes to the distant river below. After four hours of this, the village of Diamroi appeared across the Bunar Gah (*gah* meaning 'river'). A plank bridge and a steep scramble up the vertical moraine wall opposite (Mick Fowler territory) took us to the village, whose flat-roofed pueblo buildings attested the region's low rainfall. Piles of maize were drying out on the roofs; small canals, bordered with black poplar, followed the contour lines of the slopes; and here and there were orchards. Diamroi was, in all but name, an oasis in a desert.

We camped in a field of corn stubble (not recommended: the stubble spikes through the ground sheets) and were soon surrounded by small boys.

A man called Kashgar visited to say he had been a cook with Roger and Ghazala during their honeymoon in 1991. And when I say honeymoon, I mean expedition. Roger had climbed the mountain with

Dave Walsh, who had come along with them. The strange thing about associative memory is that when Kashgar mentioned my friends, I immediately felt my hangover returning. His friend Mir Alam, one of our porters, put down his load to greet him, then began to gesture at us. Mir Alam was a great beast of a man with a full beard and a crew cut. This big smiling giant had no means to communicate with us other than gestures. I tried out a couple of ideas; entwined little fingers in East Turkestan means marriage. It worked here too. Mir Alam was married. A universal sign for little boy is a bent forefinger pointing down: try it, you will understand at once. At this, Mir Alam chortled and nodded, holding up a Victory sign to indicate he had two sons. In Baltistan I was shown a sign for girl: spread out your hands, palms out, then touch forefingers and thumbs together. At this Mir Alam turned to the other porters and laughed out loud at this miracle of communication. It was a golden moment.

Five hours' walk above Diamroi through an impressively narrow gorge is the group of hamlets marked on our map as Zangot, but known locally as Jel, with Ser being the main village in this group.

In Ser, we camped on more corn stubble (doubly not recommended) and our twelve Diamir porters demanded a goat as advance *baksheesh*. These charming porters had already taken, for three days' work, the same wages as a Balti is paid working the entire route from Askole to K2 base camp, a journey of six days. I looked at their guns. Rafael added Diamroi porters to taxi drivers and customs officials on his growing list of daylight robbers.

We resolved to get porters from Ser in future. Speaking to the ragged inhabitants of the ten or so households that made up the village, we asked how was it they were so different from the rest of the valley. One of them had rudimentary English and with many repetitions and hand gestures, he slowly told us their story. He said they were Khiliwals who first came from their native Kohistan three generations ago, a band of impoverished migrants eking a marginal living during the long construction of the Karakoram Highway.

They had been brought here for their expertise with road-building explosives. In return for blasting the impressive cattle trail from Diamroi to Ser, the migrants were granted land for dwellings.

Next morning Rafael made a litre of porridge for me and a gallon for himself. He saw me hesitate.

'Wik,' he said, meaning me, 'Wik, you eat less than Freya.' Freya was Rafael and his partner Camila's daughter. Despite being just two years old, she clearly had a monstrous appetite.

After Ser, at around 2,400 metres, the path climbed gently through an ablation valley on the right bank, the south-facing side of the valley, past the summer settlements of Katchal at 3,000 metres, and Kurt Gali at 3,600. Running down to the ablation valley were red buttresses of granite, gneiss or perhaps fubarite. (My geologist friends often use this acronym: Fucked-Up-Beyond-All-Recognition-ite.) They were filled with climbing possibilities: faces seamed with cracks, pinnacled ridges, arêtes and grooves, all rising out of the birch forest, now de-foliated for the winter. And all the while we climbed, white peaks took an increasingly prominent position on the horizon.

Past the Diamir Gah across the valley from us, the steep-sided gorge of the Airl Gah led towards the Mazeno Gali, or pass, at 5,400 metres, and thence down to the Rupal valley on the south-east side of Nanga Parbat. This was once A.F. Mummery's route into the Diamir valley and is now a popular trekking route.

We chose Kurt Gali as our winter base. It was still an hour's walk below the summer base camp site at 4,100 metres but had several serviceable shepherd's huts which would provide better shelter than a tent when the snows came. The summer base would become our advanced base (ABC) should we need one when trail-breaking in December. Even then, in October, it became icy the moment the sun dipped below the Mazeno ridge. To keep our base safe from casual visitors, we hired Shakar Khan to watch over the camp and cook when we returned from sorties. To keep him company, we also hired his uncle Lashkar Khan as an assistant. He was a fierce and large man, with a big black beard and a limp. The expedition was now fully underway.

On our first night in Kurt Gali, while Rafael enjoyed an excellent and deep sleep, I experienced a series of nightmares. I always sleep badly at the start of these things. Five years earlier, in 1991, Steve Sustad and I set off to climb the Karakoram peak Ultar after supper and climbed all night, partly to avoid the heat of the day but also to avoid the terrors of that last bivouac before starting. Back at home, my wife Maggie and son Hugo were moving house. Part of my dream was a memory of Hugo singing 'Yai-yai-yippie, my teacher is a hippie!' It is an effect of acclimatising that you walk with leaden limbs, sleep badly and find tunes running on an endless loop inside your head. Next day, 'Yai-yai-yippie' circled round inside my head incessantly as we made our first recce.

Walking up to summer base camp took us two and a half hours; it would later be half that with acclimatisation. Here, the glacier turned a corner, the main branch rising to the left and changing its name confusingly from Diamir to Diama. This upper glacier was a terrifying jumble of collapsing towers. The lower glacier, the Diamir, was fed entirely by avalanche and sérac debris.

That day we saw the lower part of the Kinshofer, our most likely route to the summit. It looked horribly icy. There was an approach slope, threatened a little by sérac and avalanche risk; then the first large feature, the BCC (Big Cold Couloir), rising from an altitude of around 5,000 metres to 6,000 metres. The couloir was capped by a rock band. The usual location for Camp 1 was at 5,200 metres on the right side of the BCC in a shallow wind scoop, while Camp 2 was in the rock band at 6,100 metres. Above the rock band was the low-angled but icy Kinshofer icefield, with Camp 3 on its left side at 6,700 metres. At the top of the icefield, a long traverse led rightwards under the Bazhin Gap towards the summit pyramid. In summer, Camp 4 is located at the left end of the basin and Camp 5 on the far side at 7,200 metres under the final 1,000-metre summit, which is split by a broad final couloir.

The summit rose four kilometres above us; we could not fully comprehend the enormity of our task. We needed to break the project down into mind-sized chunks, and deal with each section as a separate project, each one a major alpine winter route in its own right.

Two days later we humped our sacks up to the summer base camp, cleared away the snow and spent our first night above 4,000 metres. We were experimenting with thin sleeping bags and down suits for sleeping. During the night, Rafael told me about the last night he spent at Camp 4 on K2 before going for the top. He had arrived there with his partner Daniel, having lost a sleeping bag at Camp 3, a snow hole that had collapsed and disappeared.

'Somehow Anatoli Boukreev, that fine man, discovered we only had one bag, and he came over from his tent and gave us his sleeping bag; he slept in his down suit.' This was the same Boukreev who would save so many lives on Everest three years later.

To get a better view of the route up Nanga Parbat, we climbed to a col at 4,700 metres with a V-sign-shaped pinnacle in the centre of it: Two Finger Col. There we were greeted with majestic views of the Diamir face. The afternoon was still, and for a couple of hours the mountain looked almost benign. Rafael turned to me and said:

'Well, Wik. Conclusion so far. The Messner route? Out of the consideration. The Mummery, we do not know yet. We are unsure of how the séracs do conflict with an ascent of it. So we do not want to talk about it until we see some séracs falling. The Kinshofer? Looking wer-ry icy. The Diama, we have seen nothing yet.'

'Ain't,' I said.

'Hey?'

'"Ain't seen nothin' yet" is the correct phrase, I believe.'

The Messner route selects the most dangerous séracs on the face and traverses under all of them. The Mummery, the most attractive natural line on the face, has the advantage of enjoying more sunshine than the Kinshofer, but is threatened on both sides by unstable bands of séracs. It includes three islands of rock: the Fang, the Middle Island

and the Third Buttress. Mummery himself reached about 6,100 metres somewhere on the Third Buttress. Rafael called it the Marilyn Monroe route: good-looking but dangerous.

We hurried down as the sun sank below the Mazeno ridge, and by nightfall reached Kurt Gali, where Shakar made us a supper of *dal* and *chapatis*. We had a rest day. Rafael had a theory that a rest day must be thirty-six hours long, meaning two full nights at base. The thermometer plummeted to well below zero.

Lashkar and Shakar demanded excessive payments for each and every additional item we required. A chicken from Ser? Fifteen dollars. Eggs were two dollars a dozen. And to bring these things up from Ser? Another thirty dollars. They were likeable, but remained rogues. They would have fleeced us for our last rupee if they could. Shakar rounded off his exhortations with the phrase 'You are like!' This should have meant, 'You may pay what you prefer.' In fact, it meant, 'If you are an honourable gentleman, you will agree to our exorbitant terms because we are poor farmers and you are filthy rich westerners who can afford it.'

It is a matter of debate exactly how rich they thought we were. The two of them looked decidedly disappointed when we explained that neither of us had any goats, let alone roaming herds of cattle. Rafael completely failed to explain to them the fungible nature of bank credit.

Toiling back up the hill, we plunged thigh-deep into snow-covered undergrowth, which Rafael said was *Dryas octopetala*. It seemed just like heather to me. And, just like heather, it made snowy trail-breaking a real chore, as we carried our twenty-five-kilogram loads slowly up the hill. The ablation valley ended abruptly at the corner of the Diamir and Diama glaciers and we camped for the night.

The glacier grumbled all night long, and so did I. At any time, either my back, knees or feet were cold and unhappy. Our tent was smaller and lower than the space under my dining table. It was back-breaking to sit up, let alone cook. Sleeping on the side produced a numb arm;

on the back, snoring; on the front, suffocation. Ice crystallising from our breath sheathed the inside of the tent and encrusted the rim of our sleeping bags with ice. But worse was to come, worse than all the above added together. Because every day Rafael woke up and said:

'Ello Wik, good to be here!'

He then prepared something called *frukosträtt* for breakfast.

'Ett is a cross between muesli and porridge. Ett is wer-ry healthy!'

'Oh God, let me out of here.' I was trapped in a small tent with a madman.

'Eat! Eat! Is wer-ry healthy!'

After *frukosträtt* we crossed the glacier to the slope under the Kinshofer. Above our left flank were the tottering towers of the Diama glacier; on the right, the outfall from the Messner séracs. It was easy going, magnificent even, but nerve-wracking.

The surface of the glacier was covered in a deceptive blanket of snow, which sometimes supported our weight, sometimes plunged us thigh-deep into a leg-breaking boulder field beneath its surface. The trail-breaking was discouraging, but after two hours we had reached a leaning ice cliff with a crevasse and a gangway across it to another block of ice. Crawling across the gangway, we must have looked like ants crossing a spill of sugar cubes.

The route now eased off, but while the approach slope was easy, it was also the only part of the Kinshofer threatened by avalanche. The sun emerged from its home behind the Mazeno ridge, promising to stay with us for the next three hours. Then the snow deepened and the trail-breaking became heavier. At one point, while following the edge of an ice cliff peppered with large boulders half hanging out and waiting to fall, Rafael said:

'Wik, I need to stop and put my helmet on. I recognise this place from my dreams. I cannot remember what the dream said, but it was bad.'

All the while, our perspective on Nanga Parbat's grand scenery slowly shifted. Now we were looking up and along the summit icefield whereas earlier we had looked straight at it. Even the Mummery line was foreshortened. The colours were elemental: blue sky, black rock, white snow, grey ice.

We were aiming for the base of the Big Cold Couloir, but by 4 p.m. were still short of our target for the day. At least we were close enough to the toe of the buttresses to feel safe from the surrounding circle of séracs, which we dubbed the Fawlty Towers. Exhausted by the work, we collapsed into the first flat spot we found. It took half an hour to get the tent up; but then, brewing with two stoves (another Rafael idea), we made a dehydrated chicken thing, macaroni and coffee, and fell into a fitful sleep disturbed by the roar of collapsing Fawlty Towers on to the Diama glacier.

The following morning brought the usual insufferable enthusiasm from Rafael and a change in the weather. A thin, high cloud had spread like dry rot across the sky as we had just decided to leave the tent and visit the site of the normal Camp 1 at 5,200 metres. The plan had been to continue our acclimatisation by going on to Ganalo Peak, part of the massif and to the north of Nanga Parbat, giving it an excellent view of the Diamir face and our route.

'Wik, I think we are not making our chances on Ganalo lesser by staying another night here.' And so, we decided to climb to the site of Camp 1 before trying our luck on Ganalo.

By 1 p.m. we were at 5,000 metres and the start of the BCC. Soon afterwards, the long stretches of hard ice convinced us it would be a good idea to pitch it for a while. Camp 1 was disappointingly icy: no tent could be pitched here after all, even if in summer the site was a good one. The climbing was easy, but the descent would need care; with a big sack, that could mean abseils. It could easily take longer to descend this ground than climb it.

Back at the tent, it was a beautiful evening, with lines of distant snow-covered peaks to the west that would have us reaching for maps on our return. Was that pointy thing Tirich Mir, first climbed by the Norwegians with Tony Streather in 1950? The fungal clouds had thinned out, letting shafts of thin light reach down into the lower reaches of the Diamir valley. We sat on our sacks and made the first brews of the evening until the light faded and the cold forced us indoors.

That night it was so cold the tent pole snapped in its sleeve. Did I say the tent was like my dining table? I was wrong. It was more like trying to sleep in a small freezer cabinet. The hoar frost inside made all movement unpleasant. After breakfast (a litre of porridge each) we carried the small tent up to stash it at Camp 1 behind a fang of rock before returning to base, where Shakar had made *dal* and *chapatis*, even though Rafael didn't eat *dal*.

We discovered a new resident, walled into a small hole in the kitchen, clucking sourly: Chantecler. The next morning we woke to the sound of Chantecler squawking his head off. He did not just announce dawn; cock-crow began well before it and continued until late morning, like one of those alarms you need to throw at the wall.

Breakfast was followed by football, which Shakar Khan and I lost 3–1 to Rafael and Lashkar, who cheated by being better at football than us. Afterwards Shakar whetted the kitchen knife and prepared lunch.

After eating Chantecler, we had a bouldering competition, in which the losing football team regained their self-respect. Shakar had a real talent for rock climbing: twenty feet above the ground and barefoot, he was turning out French 6b moves. The granite bouldering was dispersed, but very, very good. In my diary the next day I wrote:

Rather missed the cock-a-doodle-doo of Chantecler this morning.
Conversation at breakfast had a grammatical side to it:
    Shakar: *Dal misho? [Dal is good?]*
    Rafael: *Dal kacho! [Dal is bad.]*
    Shakar: *Mashi [honey] mishi?*
    Rafael: *Mashi mishi!*
    Victor: *Chawal? [Rice?]*
    Shakar: *Chawal mishi!*

Victor: *Chawal mishi, dal misho?*

Shakar nods.

Victor: *Ah, Rafael, see the adjective agrees with the noun in some way. Let's try gender. Chawal woman, dal man?*

Shakar: *Yes, yes, mashi woman. Mashi mishi. Chawal woman, dal man. Dal misho.*

Rafael: *Wik, the grammar is all very good, but do you think he understands I don't eat dal?*

The Shina lesson over, Rafael demonstrated his dubious musical talents with a Danish song.

Denmark: nul points.

The wind shifted round to the south and snow plumes drifted in pennants from the summit ridge of the Mazeno wall. We watched this from our outdoor living room, a tarpaulin pinned to the earth by expedition kitbags and barrels. Rafael examined Lashkar Khan's toe; he had dropped a rock on it some weeks earlier. Layer after layer of kerosene-soaked rag was unwrapped till a blackened nail but otherwise healthy *doigt* was unveiled. For lunch, I attempted to make a Spanish omelette, which looked more like a Spanish scrambled egg by the time I had finished with it, but everyone claimed to appreciate my efforts anyway.

After lunch, Rafael packed six days of food. I packed a pair of thin climbing ropes, which Shakar and Lashkar were anxious we shouldn't leave on the mountain.

'Snow coming, many problem,' Shakar warned. 'You stay rope here.' I think they'd become quite attached to the ropes.

In the afternoon we staggered slowly towards our ABC, where we listened to a dull roaring sound during the night. There are many things this sound could have been: the background noise left in the cosmos after the big bang; a distant river buried deep beneath the glacier. The most likely explanation was winter winds tearing across the mountain's summit ridges 4,000 metres above our heads. It was most disturbing.

We now started our acclimatisation climb, aiming to reach 6,000 metres on Ganalo Peak before returning to Rawalpindi to meet our official liaison officer. The line we chose involved reaching Two Finger Col again, where we bivouacked, and then finding a line through the confusing maze of gullies and buttresses above. We weren't sure if it would go, but a promising icy gully disappeared round to our right and it led pleasingly to a fine exposed rock crest. This we followed for four pitches. It reminded me of *Eagle Ridge* on Lochnagar. While we climbed it, a massive avalanche billowed out across the lower half of the Mummery Rib. Now we knew the answer to the question of whether or not to try that line. The answer was not.

Above the crest was a section of glacier that needed a spot of front-pointing before we arrived at a big flat bivvy under a small sérac. We were now at 5,700 metres on the Ganalo ridge, and in two days had climbed 1,700 metres. Rafael constructed a small platform with typical enthusiasm. It had a spectacular position, overlooking two couloirs.

We spent a second night here, and during the evening Rafael told me about his time in Alyth. He had first stayed there in 1982 when he was nineteen years old, working for a tree nursery in Ruthven for seven months that summer, where he was introduced to Scottish drinking at the modest rate of 'twenty-five pints and two nips a week' in the company of Gordon Ingster and Doug Rennie. They introduced Rafael to rock climbing.

'It was probably the best summer of the century for climbing. It was a terrible summer for nurseries. Between May and August we probably had four days of rain.'

'Not a bad winter too,' I added.

'In those days, I used my winters for dismantling my motorcycle, drinking tea and being social. We went climbing in Lochnagar, Dunkeld, Ardverikie. That was one of the best places: classical routes, nice surroundings as well.'

In the morning, the inner tent was caked in ice, which we scraped into our cooking pots, allowing us to sit up without our necks filling with snow. The other morning routine was pulling on our inner boots an hour before the outer boots to avoid cold toes and possible frostbite. It had fallen to -18° Celsius inside the tent and -24° Celsius outside that night. This was equivalent to 8,000 metres in summer.

'We are having a good time getting used to reality,' Rafael said.

The weather sent us down, mackerel clouds spreading across the sky as large lenticular pillows sat on Nanga Parbat.

By the time we reached our old bivouac spot at Two Finger Col the sky was dropping like a leaden lid. Here, the temperature was a comfortable -15° Celsius, and by the time we had down-climbed another thousand metres to Kurt Gali, it was snowing. Although we had dispensed with the ropes, we still had to front-point down long stretches of ice. Rafael's down suit sprang a leak and he left a trail of feathers all the way to base camp.

That night it snowed heavily outside the shepherd's hut. We read, wrote and sipped Lagavulin in silence, drying out our sleeping bags, which had sprouted lumps of ice from interstitial condensation. There were rumours that a Polish team would be here in ten days, but we ignored that. Rafael read *The Tao of Pooh* in Danish. We were comfortable, semi-acclimatised and ready to embark on the next phase of the trip: our battle with Pakistani bureaucracy. The following day we went down to Ser and Diamroi and headed out for Islamabad.

After an eight-day break in Islamabad, we arrived back at Kurt Gali on 1 December having acquired our liaison officer, Ghulam Hassan. Hassan had deep-set eyes and a slow, deliberate manner. He was a mountaineer, from Hunza, and the following spring would be going with the first Pakistani expedition to Everest, to be led by the well-known climber Nazir Sabir. We had enjoyed a beautiful walk up the valley to our shepherd's hut but the stream was now a river of ice, as though photographed with a slow shutter speed. The thin birch forest showered us with snow as we brushed past, and the enticing buttresses of red rock were dusted with it, as though telling us to come back in summer. The scenery was now entirely different. There was no doubt now that this was a winter expedition.

We waded in the general direction of the Diamir glacier with Hassan. It was a little difficult to find our old track, but that didn't matter too much; this was about trail-breaking, not path-finding. As usual, Rafael charged off, and in thirty minutes was a distant speck on the horizon.

Hassan said, 'He moves really fast.'

'Yes,' I replied. 'Down here, all my climbing partners do. I have learnt to live with that.'

We had a constant trickle of visitors at base camp, in part because Shakar Khan was quite unable to contemplate the idea of being alone for a night while we were climbing.

Johar was from the impoverished village of Ser. He brought with him a Chinese rifle and said he was looking for ibex, which he never found.

'Why can't you find them?'

'Ibex are very sensible. They run away quickly.'

We asked Johar if he would collect the goat we had paid for. Then, just as it was getting dark and so too late for Johar to return safely to Ser, we had another visitor. He introduced himself as Jaba, Johar's big brother, saying he had come to see if Johar was okay. They looked like twins. Hassan said there are villages in these mountains where the entire population looked like twins.

Speaking with Johar that night, Hassan slowly drew out of the young man the sad story of his village. Three generations back, when his people were finally rewarded for the construction of the cattle path and had settled in Ser, they discovered that people in Diamroi had kept the best grazing rights for themselves. This effectively forced the inhabitants of Ser to submit to a kind of indentured labour system where, as herders, they were paid in kind. Ser earnt its keep in sheep products, butter, milk and meat. In this kind of system, the labourer typically has to borrow cash from the employer, creating a burden of debt which is rarely payed off. Hassan said it was called *payalo*, and had long since been abolished in his home valley of Hunza. And that was why Ser was so poor.

Next morning the small spring about twenty minutes above Kurt Gali was still running, but only just. I carried the twenty-five-litre container up inside a rucksack. Hassan decided to come with me, and during the walk he told me that Lashkar Khan had threatened him.

'How did he do that?'

'Lashkar said, "I am a Chilas man. We do not follow the rules of Pakistan. You better be very careful." I have to go to police. This man is really bad.'

We were not to realise how bad until much later. After the climbing was over, we persuaded Lashkar to hire the shepherds of Ser as porters, but when it came time to pay them he kept two-thirds of their earnings for himself. He lied to them about the amount we had paid and then threatened them with the loss of their houses if they talked to us. Fortunately, Hassan discovered the scam and threatened to call the police, forcing Lashkar to return most of the wages to the shepherds. But that was all to come. At this point all we understood was that the brutish Lashkar Khan was gradually replacing Shakar as the dominant force in our camp, and the inhabitants of Ser were little better off than slaves. The contrast between this human tragedy and our introverted and privileged world of mountaineering could not have been more marked.

After fetching water and avoiding any Jack-and-Jill falls down the hill, we had tea. Then we packed some Mad Cow Cheese (*La vache qui rit*), Ryvita and a packet of salami, and set off for the day towards the Diama glacier, four hours away. We got back in the evening for a supper of *chapatis* and boiled bits of goat, and paid Johar for his goat portering and Jabar for fetching more water. As we sat around the fire, Rafael carefully noted the amounts paid in his book.

'How do you spell Jabar?'

Shakar Khan leant forward in concentration and said slowly: 'Jay, Ay, Bee.'

All eyes turned on Shakar, who became shy. He had to be encouraged and coaxed on.

'Jay, Ay, Bee, AAR?' Round of applause. It was his first ever attempt to spell in English.

The time had come for our attempt. We gathered our supplies for the mountain, discovering that our high-altitude rations alone weighed eighteen kilograms. We also had eight days of low-altitude food, which weighed another twenty kilograms. I didn't know how we were going to move all that stuff up the mountain. In the end, the only solution was to build supply dumps and make multiple journeys up to the base of the mountain.

At 3.30 a.m. the next morning, we set out for the mountain. We planned to triple-carry loads to Camp 1 at the bottom of the route and then climb it. We would not be returning to base until we were done. Rafael made blueberry-soup porridge: a spoonful for me, a litre of the stuff for himself.

'All this porridge, you must be getting ready to give the mountain hell.'

'No, I am getting ready to give my body hell.'

This was a very fair summary of our little expedition.

An hour later, as we left for the Diama glacier, I was caught by an overwhelming need to defecate. My salopettes had 'round the world' zips, but not far enough round the world for me. It was dark and my head torch fell off. I was terrified I would shit on it by accident. It was -20° Celsius, and having failed to negotiate the zip, I had to take all my clothes off except my vest. Then I became anxious that the salopettes would fall into the shit with the torch. All this took ages and I was beginning to get frostbite or at least go numb when I realised I couldn't find my gloves. (I had had to take them off too, it being difficult to use toilet paper with gloves.) It was turning into one of those days.

Walking up to Ben Nevis from the golf course car park, the only way to stop the boredom is by knowing which section of the Allt a'Mhuilinn is underfoot. Similarly, here we had now walked up the glacier so many times we'd internalised names for the different sections. My favourite zone was about halfway, the site of one of the summer base camps, a snowy plain half a kilometre across, where to avoid drifts we always made tracks that described an elegant curve. This was described in my mind as the Plain of the Arcing Path. Below the Arcing Path was another plain, liberally dotted with willow bushes, black against the snow, and suggestively dome-shaped. I could not help thinking of this place as the Pubic Plain. Higher up was the Flying Wing, a fine sheltering rock where we would sometimes stop for a drink. And, higher again, a stream we called November Water.

The walk was followed by another bad night. I woke frightened, but not sure why. It did seem to be an extremely hostile environment. A little wind, some clouds, and we had to be very careful not to get frostbite. It only took a minute. Perhaps the dreams sprang from this subconscious anxiety of getting it ever-so-slightly wrong.

I had a breakfast of salami while the infernal Rafael was porridge-ing and singing 'Piddly-pai, piddly-pai'. This was Swedish for 'tiddely-pom', as in: 'And nobody / KNOWS-tiddely-pom / How cold my / TOES-tiddely-pom … ' Rafael was still reading *The Tao of Pooh*. He told me how he did his Christmas shopping serendipitously throughout the year.

'If I come around something that someone needs I buy it. When I was in Canada, I bought a kayak in bone and a hat, and kept them for Freya and Camila at Christmas. This was in August. In support of the local artists.'

'Where was that?'

'Baffin. You fly in by Fokker there as well. If you are very lucky you get Annie the stewardess. She wears overalls and looks rather tough. She has very red hair.'

Next day we had sunshine for just two and a half hours. After that the weather was perfect, with clear skies but no sun, since we were in the winter shadow of the mountain. We carried two loads up the Diamir glacier and then put the tent up at 4.30 p.m. We were desperate to get into our sleeping bags before frostbite damaged our fingers, but it still took an hour in the bitter cold.

I had another night of bad dreams. Sometimes I really wished I wasn't there. Rafael started calling the Big Cold Couloir the Dark Couloir because it never got any sunshine. It was a grey sheet of ice. Even Rafael, normally impervious to cold, was cold that night. We might as well have been living in a deep freeze. Even with two foam mats each we were losing heat to the ground. I dreamt of my family. Gap-toothed Hugo and Maggie the homemaker. Then appeared the ghost of Andy Fanshawe, killed a few years earlier on Lochnagar. Andy told me to push my freshly filled pee bottle down to the bottom of the sleeping bag to warm my toes. I followed his advice. I woke with the start of a sore throat and felt instantly depressed. To cheer myself up, I made coffee and woke the gently snoring Rafael to drink it, which he did, grumpily.

Having warmed up a bit, we broke trail slowly, using snow shoes, to a small rib above the initial icefall, a place we felt to be relatively safe from the huge sérac barriers either side of the route. We had not moved far, but we had moved a lot: a triple-carry across the glacier and up the spur. The views down the valley were beautiful and I removed my gloves for just a few minutes to take photos, knowing that people had lost their fingers doing just that.

We found a perfectly flat pond frozen into the séracs, the ideal spot for a tent. Both of us had cold feet most of the day, and with no sun to dry the sleeping bags, they had lots of ice in them. We anchored the tent not with tent pegs, but ice screws. It was perfect.

I got very cold that night on one side only, the side away from Rafael. The sleeping bags were beginning to lose their insulation as they gathered ice. All night long we were disturbed by the low rumble-crunch of séracs falling either side of our tent. Rafael reasoned that they had a ninety-eight per cent chance of missing us, so it must have been the thought of that remaining two per cent that kept waking us. We had *rotsal grytte* (root veg stew) for supper. This was the first freeze-dried meal that I had remotely enjoyed. Ever. Rafael spilt his porridge on his sleeping bag.

'Oh no! Disaster!' he said, and sprinkled raisins on the spill before spooning breakfast off the bag and into his mouth.

'You know, Wik,' he said between each spoonful, 'the answer is to use a wapour barrier sleeping bag between the down suit and the sleeping bag. That way, the down suit can dry out during the day.'

'Hmm,' I said, thinking about the state the down suit would be in after a week of that treatment.

The sleeping bags were so frozen they crunched and crackled as we straightened them out. Although the weather had been perfect, we had had no sun all day. We hoped to dry the sleeping bags when we got to Camp 1. Trail-breaking was heavy work, the snow waist-deep in places. We were exhausted by the time we reached a safe place to pitch the tent, fifty metres below where we had stored our smaller mountain tent in November. We found a site on a shoulder just right of the mouth of the Dark Couloir, calculating it should be safe from the frequent avalanche and icefall generated by the triangular sérac on the left side of the Dark Couloir. The slope was hard windslab, perfect for cutting into blocks, like styrofoam, for igloos or, in our case, tent platforms. Using these blocks, we fashioned a platform, building a buttress of snow over the abyss big enough to pitch the larger, more comfortable tent we had been using below.

The following day was another spent load-carrying. Rafael broke trail most of the way, expending enough energy to light up Gothenburg. We had been arguing about the least inefficient line. I wanted to zigzag. Rafael preferred to stomp straight up the slope under his huge pack. Just as I thought I had won the argument, a large powder avalanche poured down my zigzag line, proving him right again, annoyingly.

Rafael's toes were very cold in spite of special additions to his boots. He was using extra thick insoles, which I was worried compressed his toes too much. He had also fitted electric toe-warmers but was saving the batteries for later, since they only lasted a few hours. There was sun for half an hour, but a veil of high cloud was being drawn across the sky, and soon lenticulars hung over Nanga Parbat. Heavy spindrift began pouring down the Dark Couloir.

Having got back to the site for Camp 1, Rafael looked for our smaller mountain tent, which we had left in a deep crack behind a large (and we thought immovable) flake of granite. It should have been easy, but it wasn't there. Finally, I caught him up, and his brows were knitted with concern when he gave me the news. It seemed the granite flake had shifted and our tent had been swept out by snowslides or avalanche.

The loss of the Gemini lightweight climbing tent was serious. The original plan involved placing the heavier but more comfortable Swedish Staika tent at Camp 1 and using the Gemini higher up the mountain. The Gemini had a footprint the size of a small bed, an efficient shape to cut out of ice or snow. The Staika was circular, making it far less suitable for steep slopes. Excavating two metres into a forty-five-degree ice slope in winter would take two days.

We were at Camp 1 by 5 p.m.; the Staika was up by 6 p.m., shortly after nightfall; and we were in our sleeping bags inside the tent by 6.30 p.m. Rafael sat up inside his sleeping bag and with a big smile said, 'Time for a wee nip.' We drank straight from the little plastic bottle.

The next day we observed our usual morning ritual. At 6.30 a.m., having pretended to be asleep for the last hour in the hope that Rafael would get up first, but knowing that he too was pretending to be asleep, I cracked first. Bending like a mummified worm, I reached out for a pan to scrape the inner tent clear of hoar frost. Ten minutes later I started the first brew, putting ice and snow on the stove to melt. An hour later we had blueberry soup. Twenty minutes after that, I put on another brew to make rosehip soup to go with muesli. At 7.40 a.m., an hour after first turning on the stove, I started another brew for tea. During breakfast, I asked Rafael a question.

'Why do you not take milk in your porridge?'

'Milk gives me burning the thrott, catarrh, and makes me shit small balls. I don't have to use anti-acids when I don't use milk ... Oh shit! Shit! Pass me your spoon, I have dropped mine in the blueberry soup.'

At 8.30 a.m. I pulled my frozen vapour-barrier socks on to my bare feet. A quarter of an hour later I began warming my inner boots inside my down jacket to clear them of frozen condensation. I'd already retrieved them from the bottom of my sleeping bag, which was icier than ever. The fact that they were frozen meant the temperature at the bottom of my sleeping bag was below freezing. At 9 a.m. I pulled on my inner boots, then my outer boots and went for a shit. By 9.30 a.m., three hours after stirring, we were ready to start climbing.

It was yet another load-hauling day, as we brought up the last of our supplies to Camp 1. Then we looked some more for the Gemini. Without it, we faced a hard choice. We could stick with the Kinshofer and see if we could reach Camp 2 in a day, where we could use the Staika tent. We could go down to base camp for another tent, except we couldn't because it would take too much time. We could switch routes to the Diama glacier. We had twelve days of food, including six days of high-altitude rations. Rafael had cold feet (physically; I had psychological cold feet) and a very cold sleeping bag. He made a mistake in bringing a -12° Celsius bag. Mine was rated at -30° Celsius. It weighed more but didn't consist of two sheets of nylon with ice lumps between them, as Rafael's did. We opted for the Dark Couloir. That night, we ate the last six slices of Italian salami. It was our big treat. We were now beginning to feel permanently hungry.

Next morning was not a porridge day. Rafael produced frighteningly healthy Scandinavian things, which looked as if they belonged in a fodder bag. This one claimed to be fruit compote with oats.

'What is this?'

'Wik, it is what the Swedish military eat for breakfast.'

'What is it called?'

'Morning dish.'

'Oh I say, that is really very informative.'

Above Camp 1, it took two hours of slowly sidestepping up the wind crust, and plunging knee-deep into soft slabs of snow, to reach the beginning of the ice. The Dark Couloir felt eerie. At first it was very quiet, with just the tinkling of ice and the occasional small pebble. The walls either side encouraged a slight echo. The ice itself was generously peppered with pebbles and rocks, many of them precariously perched on stalks of ice where the receding snows had left them exposed. This made for very careful rope-handling.

At first there was no sign of any fixed rope, then after a couple of pitches an old piece of blue and another of yellow cord appeared out of the ice. These fragments were tied off to loose pegs. This was no surprise: in winter the cold causes differential expansion, and winter pegs in the Alps are commonly loose. Some of the rope had been scarred by rockfall, and that was rather ominous, though we didn't realise at first just *how* ominous.

We had been going three hours, ice climbing on tiptoes, the ice no more than fifty-five degrees at its steepest, but iron hard, so that a fraction of an inch was all that the axes and crampons could penetrate. This meant that we not only had to pitch the ice, but also place runners.

I reached a little bay with finger-width cracks, where a bit of blue rope was tied off to a red Cassin peg and a Chouinard Lost Arrow. I pulled both of them out with my forefinger, repositioned them in the cracks and then hammered them back up to the eye. I had just retied the Lost Arrow when there was a sound above me, a sound that more than any other makes my hair stand on end and chills my soul. A kind of fluttering, like the air-cooled engine of a VW Beetle, interspersed with explosive crunches. A large flock of stones was flying down our route, the bigger ones crashing into ledges and outcrops, sending down showers of splintered ice and shards of stone. One lump the size of a man's head smashed into our last belay and ricocheted out into the white again. Then another group of stones fell past. In all, the stonefall lasted for a couple of minutes, but it felt like hours, and when it was over I was left shaking. I shouted to see if Rafael was okay below me.

I stayed at that belay for over an hour, while Rafael followed the pitch then led another above it, hugging the right wall to avoid any more rockfall. And in that hour, my hands and toes began to chill. At 4 p.m. we took the decision to retreat from the Dark Couloir, which we did in the dark, pulling the abseil ropes very carefully indeed, so as not to disturb all those rocks and pebbles half stuck in the ice.

The stonefall was only one part of our decision not to press on with the Kinshofer line, but it was an important one.

That night at Camp 1 we had a long discussion in the tent. It was now obvious that we would need either masses of fixed rope or several tent platforms to climb the Dark Couloir. The fixed rope we simply did not have, and the tent platforms would have been hard enough to cut in the ice with the Gemini, but with the round Staika it was impossible to find suitable sites in the couloir. And then there was the stonefall.

That night I fell asleep as Rafael continued talking, thinking aloud about how we could have approached the Dark Couloir differently.

'Supposing we give a damn [he meant 'Supposing we don't ... '] about stonefall, we could bivouac a short night sitting on a ledge. With two fifteen-hour days we could reach the col.'

I was too tired to reply.

In the morning we had a late start. It felt like a holiday. Almost.

There was the usual morning ritual: scrape, brew, pee, struggle. Rafael lost his gloves inside his sleeping bag, as well as his spare clothes.

'The next thing I am looking for is the black bag of clothing.' Such is the 'day-after' nature of organisation.

'I think I slept on the bivvy brush, and now it is out of shape ... '

'Do you see my mug? I had it here and now it is gone.'

It was behind him. It's a curious thing about tents: the smaller they are, the harder it is to find things.

Rafael was still talking. 'The reason I am feeling very insecure about this venture is my boots. I definitely need overboots outside. Hands,

I think we have gloves that work, but we have to work with overgloves. Well, let's go and have some fun double-packing the loads.'

We had become quite used to living in a tent at -25° Celsius. It was going to be too warm at Kurt Gali.

Back at our ABC, the summer base camp, we rested after the last long carry down. We had whole-body tiredness, having had no rest days or warm nights for ten days. We sat, half crouching under the small tent with aching backs. We passed each other pistachio nuts, forgetting that the salt would work its way into our cracked fingers, which made us wince when it did. As planned, we had given our bodies hell.

The next day, Rafael and I tried to climb a ridge overlooking the Diama glacier, with a view to attempting a quick sortie. We were just too tired. With all the triple and double carries from base camp, this was now our twelfth day without rest. We had not seen the sun for most of those days. We sat exhausted on an outcrop and looked down the Diamir valley towards Kurt Gali, Ser and beyond that to Diamroi. There was an incredible array of cloud patterns drifting over. Hockey sticks. Sand ripples. Mare tails. Every pattern I had ever seen just drifted over, as if the clouds were bored of keeping to just one shape. We enjoyed the scene, and rested. It was the end of our expedition. The unequal struggle was over, and at last we had a few moments to do nothing but look at the mountains and clouds.

10

GUIDING LIGHTS

(1996–2012)

GEORGE THE ADVENTURER (1921–1952)

After the Nanga Parbat thing with Rafael, my life began to change. It was, I suppose, some kind of mid-life crisis, though as far as I can tell, the crisis began long before and has continued ever since. I gave up full-time architecture for mountain guiding, struggling through a set of exams more demanding than the ones I had taken twenty years earlier. I moved to the Chamonix valley, while Maggie remained in Scotland. I wrote to Nick Kagan to say I had become a guide and received a reply to say he had done the same thing.

My father, George, would never accept that his eldest son had become a mountain guide, which he thought of as being some kind of manual labourer. He still introduced me to his friends as 'my son the architect'. George was a man of contradictions: open-minded and opinionated, a believer in the equality of all men and at the same time a terrible snob.

My father was the son of a Jewish father and Catholic mother. Their religion was significant because he was born in Munich in 1921, during the Weimar Republic. His younger brother, Hans-Peter, arrived at the height of hyperinflation, but despite this the brothers enjoyed a privileged upbringing. Educated by Jesuits at Kolleg St Blasien in the Black Forest (excellent rock-climbing site, by the way) they returned home for summer holidays by Tegernsee and winter skiing under the Wallberg, where their grandmother kept a house. Meanwhile, on a bigger stage, political wheels were grinding on. After the Nazis seized power in 1933, the British prime minister Ramsay MacDonald offered sanctuary to Kurt Hahn. Settling near Ramsay MacDonald's hometown of Lossiemouth, Hahn founded Gordonstoun School, based on the philosophical ideas he developed in his German school, Schloss Salem, his rather Teutonic interpretation of the English public-school system (morning runs, cold showers); and he would later create the Outward Bound movement. Hahn in turn arranged for George's Jewish father, my grandfather Victor, to escape in 1936. The rest of the family followed a year later, the first of many escapes in George's life.

Hahn collected not only pupils from this German exodus, but also teachers. Two sisters, Frauen Margarete Hoff and Suzanne Lachmann, taught music; Dr Richter taught biology; and George's parents, Victor and Traudl, taught riding to pay for their children's tuition. Although George excelled in sports, the German side of him never seemed to grasp the most basic rules of cricket. 'On whose side are those two men in white coats?'

Not all the teachers were immigrants. In 1938 George's housemaster was Freddy Spencer Chapman, fresh from his Himalayan odyssey, having made the first ascent of Chomolhari, the iconic mountain at the corner of Sikkim, Bhutan and Tibet. This was, for about a month, the highest summit ever trodden by man. Chapman was famously tough, surviving a capsized kayak in his polar exploration with Gino Watkins, whose own kayak can still be seen in the Royal Geographical Society. In 1937 on Chomolhari, Chapman ran out of climbing partners until only the Sherpa Pasang Dawa was left for the summit. This was the same Pasang Dawa who climbed the Bottleneck rocks on K2 with Fritz Wiessner two years later. After teaching at Gordonstoun, Chapman spent three years behind enemy lines in the Malayan jungle, much of that time working closely with Chinese communist guerrillas. This intellectual adventurer had a profound influence on the young George, and he was to remain a friend and influence the direction of George's life again fifteen years later.

With the outbreak of war, George was given the choice of internment in Canada or joining the Pioneer Corps, digging latrines for the British army. He chose the latrines and immediately set about his seniors with demands to be transferred to a combat unit. His somewhat naive idea was that he would be sent to the Asian theatre. Chapman was already there, so why not? Predictably, the military posted George to the one service that would make him seasick. Not only that, but as a German-speaking Royal Marine commando, his services would be required in Europe, not Malaya. He also had to change his surname. Saloschin was too obviously German. This being the army, the choice was simple: Smith or Saunders. And since he was not permitted to add a silent P to just plain Smith, he selected the marginally less proletarian Saunders. Of the next few years, George said, 'It was the most exhilarating time I have ever had in my entire life.' His unit operated in small teams of two and three, running raids into continental Europe, often parachuting in by night and extracting themselves by sea. They caused general mayhem, brought back military documents and, on one occasion, captured enemy officers.

On 6 June 1944, 45 Royal Marine Commando took part in Operation Overlord under Brigadier Simon Fraser, Master of Lovat. George once said his company suffered ninety per cent casualties in the first twenty-four hours of D-Day. The unit fought on to Merville, where he was wounded in a grenade attack taking cover behind a column. He'd left his leg sticking out and it took the shrapnel. In the next few days he was captured no less than three times, escaping back to his unit each time but one. His final capture led to a lengthy sojourn as a POW in Germany, escaping only to fall into the hands of the Russians and their labour camps. From there he escaped once more to make his way to the Ukrainian seaport of Odessa and finally back to England a year after D-Day.

The few published histories give his story in the barest detail. George was mentioned in dispatches and recommended for, but not awarded, the Military Medal. None of these accounts can convey his bravery: exhausted, wounded but fighting on for a better world for us to live in. George rarely talked about his wartime experiences; he lost most of his companions and came to believe that God had a personal role in bringing him back alive from each sortie.

By 1948 George was in Hong Kong working for the extremely wealthy father of his English fiancée. Hong Kong was wonderful for George. He borrowed a Rolls-Royce, went rock climbing (he was injured in a soloing fall), demonstrated parachuting with an umbrella (broke his arm), and generally seems to have been gadding about. While his arm was in plaster, he met eighteen-year-old Russian emigrée Raiza Popova, and married her. That put an end to the job with his ex-fiancée's father, and led to a return to Europe and the beginning of our family.

The Hong Kong sojourn was followed by a period of unemployment, broken by a stint of ski instruction in St Anton and helping out with PE at Gordonstoun. His next break came in 1952, when Freddy Spencer Chapman recommended him for a special forces unit countering the Malayan communist insurgency; the self-same communist guerrillas that had once aided Chapman against the Japanese were now the enemy. George arrived in Singapore to find that Chapman had resigned from the army. Undaunted, George wangled a transfer to the police, where he rose to the rank of superintendent.

Some of my earliest memories are from our house on Scotts Road. There was a gentle, asthmatic former racehorse called Sunhora that could be ridden by our mother, and a vicious animal called Naru that George somehow tamed and trained into a polo pony.

Things got even better for George when he was offered the post of comptroller of the royal household for Sultan Abu Bakar, fourth sultan of the third-largest state in Malaysia, Pahang. And that is how we came to be in Pekan. When I told George about finding Aziza again, he replied:

'And did you have a meeting with Sultan Ahmad Shah? You remember? He is the son of Abu Bakar.'

'No. I don't think I remember anything about their highnesses. The person I remember best is Aziza.'

'Oh, what a pity. You should have met Sultan Ahmad.'

My mother's reaction was more normal. I was driving from Scotland to France. Mum lived in Wandsworth, a good halfway stop for a cup of tea before heading for the Dover ferry.

'Oh, that is very nice. Have you got a photograph of Aziza?'

'I haven't,' I said.

'Can you get the box down from the attic? It is heavy for me.'

The box of old photograph albums was just behind the trapdoor to the attic. Standing on a chair, I lifted the cardboard box down. Over tea and biscuits we pored over fading black and whites of Singapore and of Pekan. There was Sunhora, Mum looking tiny on top of the fifteen-hand stallion. And here was the magistrate's house on stilts by the football field. There were several of George, looking young and handsome, and two small children who also appeared in Mum's small oil-paint portraits.

Half an hour went by all too quickly and I became anxious about making the next ferry. Only I couldn't find the car keys. That took me another hour. I retraced my steps assiduously until I found them. In lifting up the attic trapdoor, I had put the keys behind the trapdoor lip in order to pick up the box of photos.

As I left, I said, 'I hate this growing old thing, Mum.'

'You're not old. What are you saying?'

'Well, first your eyesight goes and then … '

'And then what?'

'The brain. Losing keys like that. It's awful. I keep forgetting things.'

'Don't be so silly,' she said. 'You were like that when you were twelve years old!' Then she gave me a big hug and pushed me out the door.

A LESSON ON THE TRIENT GLACIER (1996)

Guiding is the art (there is little science in this profession) of looking after people in big mountains. However, the art of it remains a bit of a mystery to me even now. I was taught by guides who would later become my peers.

As one of my mentors, Pete asked if I would accompany him as an aspirant guide, the guiding version of an intern, to climb some small summits around the Trient glacier. Pete was an imposing senior guide, who became marginally less so after his morning coffee and cigarette.

The weather didn't work out. The couple Pete was guiding were not having the most interesting day. We'd trekked across the Trient Plateau under an overcast sky, reaching the bergschrund of the Aiguille du Tour at the same time as the clouds. The easy scramble led to a summit with no view. It began to snow gently. We trekked back across the glacial plateau to the Col d'Orny, where the weather began to clear up a bit. The Orny glacier, like a dirty white carpet leading down to Champex, was shrinking fast, like all Alpine glaciers. But it had – has still – a field of crevasses 200 metres beneath the col. Looking at the crevasses gave Pete an idea.

'Let's give them a bit of excitement to end the day.'

'Good idea. What do you plan?'

'Crevasse rescue,' he said with a twisted smile.

'Really?' I was already beginning to have doubts.

'You go first across the crevasse field.'

'And then?'

'You fall in and I rescue you.'

'Are you sure? What if you … ' But it was no use. Pete had made up his mind. If I wanted my logbook signed off, I would have to do as I was told. And definitely not suggest that I was worried about the rescue.

I walked down towards the crevasse field wishing I were somewhere else. The snow cover was thin. In many places, bare glacier ice bulged out of the wind-scoured snow. Behind me, on the rope, was Pete. Tied into the rope behind him were the clients, watching with interest. I prayed Pete was paying attention. He was larger and heavier than me, which was a good thing; he should be able to halt my headlong plunge with inertia. And that was my last thought before the rope linking me to Pete popped tight. I threw myself to the ground to stop myself being dragged backwards towards a small round hole in the snow where Pete should have been. On the other side, the clients were also lying on the ground, also having been dragged towards the hole.

'That's odd,' I said to myself as I scraped out the top layer of loose snow to drive in an ice screw. Why had he broken through the snow bridge I had just trudged over? I didn't think he was *that* much heavier than me. Then, having fixed the anchor, I crawled to the edge of the hole. Inside, the crevasse opened up like the dome of a cathedral. It was huge, with beautiful icicle chandeliers and a thin blue light. Pete was dangling like a caterpillar on a thread, turning round and round. As he slowly spun in circles, shaking the snow from his head, he berated me for not taking the fall. 'It should have been the sodding aspirant ... it should have been the sodding aspirant ... ' Every time he swore, clouds of exhaled breath billowed out like the speech bubbles of a cartoon.

I crawled back to the ice screw and hauled him up, only to find we now had two guides on one side of the crevasse and two clients on the other side. It was beginning to look like one of those days. On the other hand, Pete really had succeeded in adding a little spice to the day. Plus, having been successfully rescued, he could hardly not sign off my logbook, no matter how annoyed he was with me.

THE MATTERHORN AND GLOBAL WARMING (2003)

By the turn of the century, I was leading treks and climbs in the Himalaya and filling up the summer season with guiding in the Alps. This was my new life. It wasn't planned; it just happened that way.

I made a contract with myself: I would continue to climb as an amateur. I would climb for the sheer pleasure of it. I would climb for the sense of satisfaction and self-worth. This contract was centred on the idea that the passion and enthusiasm for the activity was what I had to offer the climbers who hired me. And if the guiding should become so routine that the passion was gone, I would return to architecture. But somehow, the guiding life never became routine. I was unfailingly hired by interesting, if not eccentric, climbers. The routes we climbed were often new to me, providing interesting problems to solve on sight. Even the normal routes on popular mountains were often filled with incident as the mountains evolved in tune with a changing climate.

In 2003 I was in Switzerland with Craig Higgins. We had already been on the Eiger and Mont Blanc together and he wanted to add the Matterhorn to complete this popular trilogy.

'It's the storming of the Bastille,' Craig said to me, looking at the climbers crowding round the first rock step.

'What?'

'It's 14 July. Bastille Day.' Craig had a keen sense of history and had correctly linked the date with the crowds.

'Ah yes,' I said, waking up a bit. It was 3.30 a.m. I had also forgotten this was exactly the 138th anniversary of the first ascent of the Matter-horn and we were following in Edward Whymper's steps.

Although Craig and I had often climbed on more remote and lonely mountains, as a mountain guide I had also got used to crowds on the handful of truly popular mountains and no longer noticed that Mont Blanc, the Matterhorn and yes, even Everest, tended to grow queues. I took it as the price of the mountain's celebrity. I would no more complain about crowds on Everest than about crowds on the London Marathon. There is plenty of lonely running and climbing to be done, if that's what is wanted.

There were traffic jams as the thirty or so teams clambering up the Hörnli ridge congregated at the initial difficult cracks. Higher up

K2

Top: The Gilkey Memorial.   **Above:** Roger Payne, me and Julie-Ann Clyma.

Below left: Anatoli Boukreev.   **Below centre:** Andrew Lock.   **Below right:** Rafael Jensen is stretchered off the mountain.

NANGA PARBAT

Above: The Diamir Face.

Right: Ganalo Peak.

Below: The Dark Couloir.

Above: Rafael on Ganalo Peak.

Left: Rafael loaded up.

Below: The real Rafael Jensen.

Maggie Saunders in the Caucasus.

George Saunders, my father.

Left: High camp on Mount Tyree, Antarctica.

Above: With Dr Rick Thurmer after Carstensz.

Below left: Everest without the queues.

Below right: Andy Parkin in Langtang.

CHAMSHEN

Above: The North Shukpa Kungchang glacier.

Left: Help arrives for Andy Parkin after our illegal satellite phone call.

Below: Andy recovers in hospital.

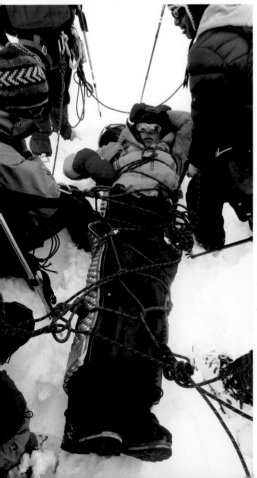

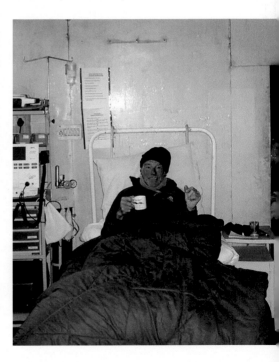

SERSANK

Above: With Mick at base camp.

Right: Mick climbing on day four.

Below: Me at the fourth bivouac.

Magnificent position; awful conditions.

The snow flutings looked beautiful, but ...

Energy-sapping ground at the foot of Chombu.

REUNITED WITH SOME OF THOSE 'UNSPEAKABLE FRIENDS'

Above: With Mick Fowler on the summit of Sersank.

Right: With Andy Parkin in Chamonix (with one of his paintings of Chamshen).

Below: Rediscovering Nick Kagan in New Zealand.

the climb, the teams became more spread out. In the dark we saw headlights, but not the climbers wearing them. Some lights were clearly off route. By dawn they would probably see the climbers on the correct route and find their way back.

From Zermatt, the Hörnli ridge looks narrow and sharp. On the mountain, it feels much more like a broad shoulder, with many possible ways past a series of obstacles, all of which have acquired local names. The route begins with three towers, after which a series of long traverses on the left side of the ridge lead to the Lower Moseley Slabs, named for an American doctor who died here in 1879. Up to this point, Craig and I had moved together. Dawn arrived. I uncoiled a bit more rope from my shoulders and led up the corner and easy slabs to the concrete base of the Solvay Bivouac Hut. Here I caught up with another Chamonix resident, Christian Trommsdorff, also guiding.

Just as we were greeting each other, there was a noise like an express train passing too close. In the half-light, I could make out falling boulders and smoke on the east face, and the peculiar odour of sulphur that accompanies rockfall filled my nostrils.

Fortunately, the Hörnli ridge divides the east and north faces. I turned to Craig and said, 'It's on the east face; we should be safe here. Funny how it always makes the smell of gunpowder.'

'The perfume of Mephistopheles,' said Craig, and as soon as he spoke, the explosion of rocks falling and ricocheting forced us to cower behind the hut.

'Is this normal?' asked Craig.

'No. Not really,' I replied. I didn't want to worry him, but I'd never in my life seen so much rock falling at one time.

After a few minutes, which seemed like an eternity (thank you, Mephistopheles), we continued to the Upper Moseley Slabs and the vertical cliffs of the shoulder, where we strapped on crampons for the final icy summit slope. Here, the first parties returning from the top passed us on their way down. We reached our summit at 8.30 a.m.

and after a brief acknowledgement to the statue of Saint Bernard, which stands just below the top, began to climb down. We took great care not to dislodge rocks or ice on to the climbers below us, and by 9 a.m. we were taking off our crampons for the descent of the shoulder.

Then Craig said, 'Listen to that!'

A long crashing rumble from the north face told of another major rockfall. This one crossed the line of the classic north face climb (no one was foolish enough to be on the north face that day) and played out on to the glacier far, far below in the shape of a huge fan. Craig and I continued down the ridge unconcerned, not having yet even begun to realise what kind of a day we were having.

By 10.30 a.m. we were back at the Solvay when distant thunder and a billowing dust-cloud betrayed yet another rockfall, this time on the Hörnli ridge itself, about an hour below us at the Third Tower.

The first guide to descend that day was Zermatt-based mountain guide Gianni Mazzone. He was about to climb down the Third Tower, just 200 metres above the Hörnli hut, when the pillar of rocks crumbled and fell away beneath his feet.

Gianni radioed the rescue services and told them that not only his party, but also all the other parties on the mountain would be unable to cross the tower safely.

By 11 a.m. the helicopters of Air Zermatt had been scrambled, piloted by Fabian Zuber and Gerald Biner. They would spend the next four hours picking up climbers from above the Third Tower and depositing them at the Hörnli hut.

As Craig and I climbed slowly down, the smoking plume of rock-dust and the returning helicopters told us a major rescue was taking place. We hadn't yet realised that we were already part of it.

Reaching the Third Tower at midday, we were confronted with a strange scene. Christian and his client were waiting on a small ledge while below them groups of four climbers at a time were clipped into the end of a 'long line', a thirty-metre wire cable, at the top of which was a roaring helicopter: a Lama, the kind with an open-frame tail.

We could not see the pilot, nor could he see us. It was all done by walkie-talkie.

When it was our turn, the Lama picked us up in one bunch, the downwash cramming us together. Christian, his client, Craig and me. I felt my stomach churning as the machine slid out over the north face. It was a spectacular open-air flight, a bit like paragliding, except above us was not a canopy but the underside of a clattering, vibrating, deafening machine. The other three may have enjoyed the flight, but me? Well, I'm easily traumatised, and was imagining all the things that can go wrong with two tons of screaming metal above your head.

Next day over breakfast, we were looking at the newspapers. They had several versions of the story. The British papers played up the danger of climbing the Matterhorn, as they have done ever since losing a peer of the realm there in 1865. The French blamed the recent heatwave and went on to focus on how it would seriously threaten wine production in the south. Meanwhile, the Swiss papers put the cost of the mass rescue at 30,000 Swiss francs and wondered who should pay for it.

'Everyone was insured, weren't they?' As he often did, Craig asked the innocently subversive question.

'They were not expecting to pay out on sixty-four rescues in one day,' said Christian, who happened to be passing by at that moment. He pulled up a seat and ordered coffee and croissants and continued. 'It's the permafrost.'

'Explain, please.'

'It is normally at 3,000 metres on the north sides. But now it is melting above 3,400 metres. *C'est le réchauffement climatique.*'

Christian leant back in his chair, bits of croissant flecking his black climbing pants. Like me, he had had a previous profession. Christian used to be an engineer. I suppose he too was in the throes of his extended midlife crisis. We looked up at the Matterhorn: that calm, stately pyramid of rock and ice; that immovable object, which we knew on closer inspection to be violently eroding away. If the mountains were disintegrating, then so was our work. I suspect we had the same thoughts. How long would it be before climbing in the Alps became an exotic and rare pastime? How long before the *réchauffement climatique* made guiding untenable? How long before we would have to go back to our old professions?

CARSTENSZ AND THE WRONG SUMMIT (2011)

Climate change was impacting mountains in the most unlikely of places, including the highest peaks in Australasia, in equatorial Indonesia. My fourth expedition there began in 2010 with a chance conversation in Sam's Bar in the Kathmandu tourist district of Thamel, a favourite watering hole for climbers returning from the big mountains. Dr Rick Thurmer had just got back from Everest, where he had performed heroics in the rescue of Bonita Norris, bringing her down from the South Summit singlehandedly before a team of Sherpas joined him at the Balcony.

Slurping his Everest beer, Rick mentioned in passing that he wanted to climb the three highest peaks in West Papua, a province of Indonesia previously known as Irian Jaya. The three also happen to be the highest peaks in Indonesia, Australasia, Oceania, the Western Pacific rim and doubtless other undefined regions too. Consequently, they are a part of the Seven Summits lists. I don't usually go in for lists, certainly not long ones, because the seemingly endless reiteration of the same thing quickly becomes boring. Yet this short list offered a good reason to travel to an unusual and interesting place with little in the way of repetition.

The three highest peaks in West Papua are Carstensz Pyramid (4,884 metres), Sumantri (4,820 metres), and the unpronounceable Ngga Pulu (4,817 metres). This last one used to be number two until its glacial snow-dome began to melt. Sumantri and Ngga Pulu now share the remains of the fast disappearing North Wall glacier, which confusingly lies on their south sides. In 2006 I had climbed Ngga Pulu, then the second highest, now the third. This time our target would be Sumantri – now the second, previously the third.

There are three ways to access the Carstensz group. The simplest, in theory, would take a few hours, through the Grasberg mine west of the peak, *grasberg* being the Dutch for 'grass mountain'. The mine, leased and operated by Freeport, is now a mile-wide hole in the ground easily seen from space, and the biggest producer in the world of gold and the third-largest of copper. The mine has a recent operating history as environmentally controversial as it is profitable. To keep out curious visitors, Freeport has prohibited travel through the mine to reach the mountain. This is a great pity because relations with native Papuans make it difficult and dangerous to approach the mountain passing close to the mine from the short access south side.

A second route, from the north, involves a six-day jungle trek from the village of Sugapa. This has many disadvantages, not least of which is the jungle. This is now the normal approach. The third route, and the one we chose this time, is by helicopter, arranged through our excellent local agent and fixer, Stephen Liew. Though expensive, it would allow us to complete the entire expedition in two weeks instead of four. Like battles, all expeditions have a starting line, and for ours there was a choice: Bali or Jakarta. Although when I say 'choice', what I mean to say is, we started at Bali.

Old climbers have a very short attention span. So, while having every intention of looking up Carstensz expedition reports in the library, I found myself leafing through a worn copy of *New Scientist*. Nothing unusual there. But something in particular caught my attention: the summary of a paper on laboratory rats. They had been given a popular asthma drug and somehow this had reversed what researchers had dubbed Age-Related Forgetfulness (ARF). After six weeks, older rats were finding their way through the laboratory maze as well as the young ones, showing that old rats can learn new tricks. The magic ingredient was a drug called Montelukast, a leukotriene receptor antagonist, and a longstanding anti-asthma drug.

I decided it didn't really matter that six rat weeks might be the equivalent of several human years; I just wanted to join the lab rats and regain my memory. On top of which, of course, I am asthmatic. So, after several false starts and wrong turns, I eventually remembered the way to my GP. In my head I had various elaborate explanations for my new-found desire to become an experimental animal. I needn't have bothered. Dr Natalie is friendly but firm. I think that it was in order to halt my absent-minded and long-winded rambling about why I wanted to try the new regimen that she prescribed Montelukast for my asthma and asked if that was all.

A week later, on 15 August 2016, I was on my way to Bali. The Qatar cabin crew were delightfully patient, serving endless rounds of drinks and cheering us with smiles when the children across the aisle refused to sleep. The man next to me snored. I can never sleep on planes, so I drank the weak beer and watched the screen. The best film was 42. Not the Douglas Adams '42', but the true story of the first black player to break the baseball colour barrier. The film gave a somewhat ageing Harrison Ford and his lopsided grin a supporting role. It was great feel-good fare, but the reason I found it arresting is that my climbing partner, Dr Rick, can from a certain angle and in the right light appear to be almost the doppelganger of Ford, the doctor's own lopsided grin giving me the curious sensation that I'm climbing with the Hollywood actor himself.

From Bali, Harrison Ford and I flew to West Papua, where torrential rain delayed our flight to base camp by two days. Then, on the third morning and rather abruptly, we found ourselves dumped by helicopter under the north face of Carstensz. The idea was to start with Sumantri, via Ngga Pulu, and then move on to Carstensz itself. A pile of bags and boxes needed to be transformed into base camp, and we needed to get going on the first objective as soon as possible. The rain was threatening to return in force. Our cook and sometime engineering student, Arleen, made tea. Armed with a bar of chocolate and carrying umbrellas, Rick and I hurried north for Ngga Pulu. First we climbed out of the Yellow valley, traversing the small ridge separating it from the Dabu Dabu valley. Splitting a pair of copper-blue lakes – *dabu* means 'lake', so *Dabu Dabu* is two of them – the path rose eastwards before turning north towards the valley's north side, then continued east for an hour or so, reaching a high col before following easy slabs back north to the summit. It was now six years since I had last climbed Ngga Pulu and I had forgotten all of this, so when a new trail led enticingly up into the mists I had a blinding moment of Reverse ARF: Reverse Age-Related Forgetfulness being the condition of remembering things that have not yet happened. So it was that I recognised this path, despite never having seen it before. And when features I didn't recall turned up, for example the lines of burly cliffs barring all upward progress, I assumed I was sinking back into normal ARF and had simply forgotten something else I should have recognised.

The path continued to thread its way through impressive karst scenery, deep intersecting canyons of limestone that formed, in essence, a giant maze, one that I was going to find hard to learn. From the confusing central canyons, a deep yellow ravine led to the snout of a tropical glacier. In the mist we could not determine from which summit it flowed and it didn't seem at all familiar. Instinct led us to a scree slope to the west, our left, where we discovered a slightly smaller but equally confusing maze of limestone canyons, then a second glacial tongue. The glacier above us would lead to something, we were sure, but exactly what was hidden in the mists.

Crampons on, and staggering upwards in the fog, calf-deep in wet snow, we passed over heat-weakened snow bridges, all the while marvelling at this equatorial glacier. And as we plodded uphill we became increasingly sure that we were nowhere near our intended mountain.

Then, out of the clouds, rose a tower of rock.

'This isn't Ngga Pulu,' I said miserably. 'Neither is it Sumantri.'

We poked round the back of the tower to see if there was a likely-looking route to the top. A moat-like canyon surrounded the tower like a castle, filled with clouds and doom, impassable with the small amount of equipment we had brought. We headed back down, following our tracks, hoping for better weather the next day, arriving back at base exhausted from the altitude. A less forgetful team would have prepared themselves with a little pre-acclimatising or Diamox. We had been to almost 5,000 metres from sea level without either. We were dehydrated and hungry, but Arleen fed us well with tea, rice and curry, and next day we left at dawn.

Being a good experimental rat, I had taken my asthma drugs in the hope I would remember a bit more about the Carstensz climb than I had about the one up Ngga Pulu. And it went well: when dawn arrived we were already halfway up the big long slabs and fixed ropes that lead to the summit ridge. The Grasberg mine was now less than three miles away; we could hear the grinding machinery, with the occasional loud rumble which in other mountains might have signified avalanches. It was turning into a blue-sky day. The limestone was dry and someone had replaced the old, frayed fixed lines with new static rope. It all felt very good.

The Carstensz summit ridge is a straightforward scramble with one awkward notch that used to involve a short rappel and then a stiff little climb up the other side. A few years ago, the notch was turned into a Tyrolean traverse. This year someone had set up a three-strand rope bridge. The bridge was no less terrifying than the Tyrolean but much easier and quicker. We arrived at the summit of Carstensz in perfect weather in just four hours from base camp. Looking south, the coast was concealed behind low-lying fog; the huge Grasberg mine was churning noisily to the west; while in other directions, the vastness of New Guinea's highlands and jungle stretched away to the blue horizon.

To the north were the peaks of Sumantri and Ngga Pulu, with their glacial apron. The weather was so clear we could spot yesterday's tracks in the snow. And then it dawned on me. While looking for Ngga Pulu, we had turned back just under the summit of our second objective, Sumantri. I felt sheepish.

'Rick,' I said, as if there was anyone else to speak to, 'you know how people are often mistaken about mountains?' I was thinking of the

Cheshire Cat; Alice says she has often seen a cat without a smile, but never a smile without a cat.

'Yes?'

'Well, I have often heard of people thinking they were on the right mountain when they were on the wrong one, but I have never heard of anyone thinking they were on the wrong mountain when they were on the right one.'

Nodding sadly, the good doctor took a last photograph of himself, posing heroically on the summit, and turned to descend. Hand-rappelling the fixed lines, we were back in camp by midday. We had enjoyed uninterrupted perfect weather, a situation almost unheard of in New Guinea. Arleen had tea and soup waiting for us. We still needed to rediscover the route to Sumantri, so next day, over breakfast tea, we agreed we would follow exactly the same route from two days earlier. Despite this, within an hour we had abandoned what little discipline we had after spotting a fine-looking path that led off over some small bluffs and into a steep canyon that seemed to head in the right direction. When we joined the old path, I then failed to recognise the place we had been just forty-eight hours before. It took twenty minutes of abject confusion before I understood where I was.

'Some bloody lab rat.'

'What did you say?' the doctor asked.

'Just talking to m'self,' I replied, feeling rather glum, and then plodded off up the next canyon. Rick produced one of his lopsided Hollywood smiles. I still could not work out what it meant. Was it amusement? Or pity?

With better weather, it was easy to see the correct route through the rock tower, and easy scrambling soon brought us to the second-highest summit in Australasia. A couple of kilometres to the east was the now rocky summit of Ngga Pulu, and north of us the jungle. Rick leant over the northern edge to photograph the steep north wall of Sumantri.

'First climbed solo, by Reinhold Messner,' I said. And looking down into the abyss, we both shuddered at the thought of Messner clinging to the slimy rocks beneath us.

Cumulus clouds were now billowing up the south side, our line of descent. Sliding down the glacier, the sky had changed its mood. Hail followed by thunder and then evil lightning sent us scampering back to Arleen's cooking. Two days later we were back in Bali sipping mai tais. A young Balinese on a bicycle stopped and stared at the doctor, then asked to be photographed with him.

'You are famous!' the youth said.

'Yes, he is,' I told him, 'but please keep it quiet. We don't need to attract crowds right now.' I motioned a zip across the mouth and made him stand beside the good doctor. The youth took his selfie with Rick and went away happy, then we ordered another round of mai tais.

'I'm sorry,' I told him, 'it was the only way. He wasn't going to leave till he had his photograph.'

Rick relaxed back on his rattan chair and continued watching the tourists drift by.

'Still, I'm sure about one thing,' I added.

'Yeah?'

'I don't know if Montelukast works for Age-Related Forgetfulness. In fact, on the evidence so far I'm pretty sure it doesn't. But my asthma does seem to have gone away.'

MONT MAUDIT AND A LINGERING DOUBT (2012)

Roger Payne was laughing at me.

'Jpeg files are just lossy ... '

'Lossy?' I stared so blankly that Roger laughed again.

'It means they lose information. And when information's gone, it's completely gone!'

Roger was still grinning, eyebrows arched (he often did that), those familiar grey eyes sparkling as he tried to explain to me how my digital camera worked.

It was the evening of 11 July 2012. We were finishing our supper in the Refuge des Cosmiques, opposite Mont Blanc under the Aiguille du Midi. Roger and I were both planning to guide Mont Blanc the following day. I introduced Roger to my client, Nikki, who had climbed Everest with me four years earlier.

Roger and I had not seen very much of each other in the nineteen years since K2. He had been immersed in his career working for national and then international climbing organisations, first the British Mountaineering Council (BMC) and afterwards the International Climbing and Mountaineering Federation (UIAA). Alongside this political work, he and Julie-Ann had found time to become one of the best-known climbing partnerships in the Himalaya. I never knew where they found the enthusiasm and energy for their projects. Recently, they had settled in Leysin. I suppose taking the occasional guiding job offered Roger some welcome relief from his years administrating the BMC and the political in-fighting of the UIAA. Whatever he was doing in life, I was always impressed by his unrelenting cheerfulness.

'It's funny, isn't it,' I said after a while, 'how that K2 team all ended up working as mountain guides?'

'I didn't put you off?'

'Actually, no. I think you gave me the encouragement and inspiration to keep at it until I qualified.' Before he could react, I continued, 'If the Payne can do it, anyone can!' It is very important not to praise your friends; it only encourages them.

We chatted about the past. About my ridiculous winter trip to Nanga Parbat. About Roger and Julie-Ann's first ascents in China and Sikkim. And about how terrible the internal politics in the UIAA had become. Finally, we talked about our plans for the following day. Roger's first intention had been to climb Mont Blanc from the Italian side.

'I was going to go via the Gonella hut, but the weather forecast wasn't good enough. So we switched round to this side.'

'Yup, it's a long way from the Gonella. What time are you starting tomorrow?' I asked.

'One o'clock breakfast.'

'Back the same way?'

'Yes, want to be in Chamonix tomorrow. You?'

'Nikki and I were going to go later, not really sure about the weather recently. Then again, we'll probably go with you. Good to be with friends.' I turned to Nikki. 'Is that okay?'

Just before one o'clock, I made the sleepy shuffle down the hut steps to the boot room, past the benches and racks of mountain boots, which smelt of damp leather and feet, past the ropes and axes hanging from the wall and pushed the entrance door open. There was no wind. The black sky was sprinkled with stars.

'Damn! No excuses.'

I woke Nikki quietly, trying to not wake others in the dormitory as well. Still shivering from the transition from warm bed to cold night air, we queued for breakfast. I didn't see Roger in the dining room. Standing there, I felt something wasn't quite right.

'Nikki, could you hold my place in the queue for a minute, please?'

The boot-room entrance I'd first looked out of faced east. I wanted to check the west-facing dining-room entrance: perhaps that would give me more information? When I opened the door, there was a sharp gust and then a steady but strong westerly breeze. The east side of the building had been wholly sheltered from this wind, which had been blowing from the west on and off for several days. There was now a niggling doubt in my head. The north face of Maudit was bowl-shaped and, as I thought about it, I pictured snow blowing across its higher slopes. I began to imagine wind-slab building up on its right-hand side. I closed the door and pulled Nikki out of the queue, apologising to Laurence, the hut *guardienne*.

'*Il faut manger plus tard, désolé.*'[4] She nodded with good-natured fake-grumpiness.

'Let's have the later breakfast at three,' I told Nikki. She nodded.

---

4   'We'll have to eat later, sorry.'

'I want to be able to see Maudit in daylight before we cross under it.' I imagined she was thinking this was typical procrastination on my part. It was lucky she knew my indecisive style from Everest. With another client, I might have felt pressure to stick to the plan. We went back to the dormitory to doze uncomfortably, waiting for the next alarm.

By 5.30 a.m. Nikki and I had just reached the shoulder of the Tacul at around 4,000 metres. The dawn light was brightening by the second and we stopped to switch off our headlamps. We should have been able to see the first group, the one o'clock breakfast crowd, two hours ahead of us. But I couldn't see anyone on the far side of Maudit. At first I assumed they were all very quick and had already gone over the top of the col and were now well on their way to Mont Blanc and out of sight. Then I noticed something, a small wriggling shadow at the bottom of the Maudit slope.

'Looks like someone has taken a fall,' I said.

Then I noticed there were in fact several shapes moving on the lower part of Maudit. I then saw there was debris at the bottom of the slope. It looked like avalanche debris. What we were seeing slowly sank in. I was watching the survivors of an avalanche, some of whom were already on their way back. I took out my cellphone and called the emergency number for the PGHM, the Chamonix rescue team.

By now, other guided teams had arrived on the Tacul shoulder. Some people turned around there and then, descending with their clients. Others decided to go and help the rescue.

I did a slightly odd thing. I sat down and pulled out the thermos flask.

'Just five minutes. Let's see what's going on.'

While we sat and watched, trying to understand the situation, my friend and Chamonix guide Octavio Defazio, arrived at the shoulder.

'*Moi, je vais donner un coup de main.*' But before lending a hand, he looked for someone to go down to the hut with his client.

I was about to suggest Nikki go with them, but instead I said, 'Nikki ... you're a medic.'

'Yes?'

'Would you go there with me to help?'

'I don't want to, but will if you think it's safe.'

'I think so. It doesn't look like there is more avalanche to come. It looks stable. I can't be sure.'

'Okay.'

'Are you really sure you're okay to help?'

This was not a comfortable question to ask of anyone, let alone a client. We waited a few minutes as we scanned the scene some more. As we looked, I realised I had been quite wrong about the avalanche risk. I had had doubts about the layers on the right (east-facing) flank of the north face of Maudit. But the slopes that went were on the left side, under the brow of a collection of ice cliffs.

As the only doctor on the mountain, Nikki proved invaluable. The first victim was sitting at the edge of the avalanche path. I recognised him as Daniel Rossetto, a neighbour from Les Houches and a guide. Nikki set to work performing triage: assessing who needed immediate help from those who could wait, or else were beyond it.

'Daniel has two dislocated shoulders. Leave him; he will survive.'

We left Daniel huddled with two helpers who would try to walk him to a safer place.

Next, we crossed into the middle of the avalanche track, where debris had gathered in large blocks. I kept looking up to see if anything else was going to come down. We were roped together because of the crevasses, and in this zone that could present problems.

'Nikki, we are tied to each other. If anything comes down we have to run the same way … yes?'

She simply carried on sorting through the injured climbers, determining those who could walk back to the hut and those with damage to lower limbs and backs who couldn't be moved. And then there were the bodies. There were four on the surface. Another under them.

A freezing wind picked up and blew across the immobilised injured. We made them as comfortable as possible as we waited for the rescue helicopter to arrive. Nikki worked with the few guides there to cover the injured with emergency bivouac bags and build snow walls against the wind. Klemen Gricar, a Slovenian guide and mountain rescue expert, helped coordinate the operation with the PGHM. Octavio took some of the walking injured out of the danger zone. The first helicopter arrived after an hour with avalanche dogs. At 7 a.m. the professional rescue team sent us amateurs down. It had been an hour and a half since I and other guides had called for them.

All this time, I had been looking for Roger. I hadn't seen him among the returning climbers nor the walking injured, but I thought I might have missed one or two. He was not among the immobilised victims. I saw three people apparently stranded above the avalanche break. Back at the hut, Laurence was on the verge of tears as I made my initial report. Nikki and I took the cable car down to Chamonix.

Once back in the valley, Nikki decided to leave Chamonix that afternoon. She changed her flight and I organised a transfer to Geneva airport: all these mundane tasks. I felt locked in a dream that had gone wrong. I spent the rest of the morning making calls to find out where Roger was. I couldn't understand it. I had seen almost all the folk on the mountain: dead, injured and alive. I called the PGHM. They told me to call Chamonix hospital. The receptionist there told me to call the emergency department in nearby Sallanches. When I explained to the woman why I was calling, her tone of voice became tender and consequently chilling.

'*Vous devriez appeler à nouveau le PGHM à Chamonix.*'[5]

After I'd called the PGHM again, I sat for a while. The sun had now started its descent, casting strong shadows across Chamonix. Above the roofs of the buildings, glowing in the afternoon sun, was the vast white bulk of Mont Blanc and its satellite summits, Mont Blanc du Tacul and Mont Maudit. The light had no warmth. It simply picked out the blank faces and aimless wandering of shoppers as they crossed the street, their shadows following them.

---

5   'You should call the PGHM in Chamonix again.'

11

HANGING ON A TELEPHONE

(2013)

It was late summer in 2012. I had my arm in a sling, the rotator cuff tendons on my shoulder having recently been bolted back on to the bones. I was rather looking forward to the coming ski season, by which time my bionic arm should have healed. The sudden loss of mobility meant more time with my computer and I noticed for the first time an unexpected email from a Divyesh Muni of the Himalayan Club's Mumbai section.

'Hello,' it began. 'Do you want to join us in the East Karakoram for a couple of virgin peaks?'

The email went on to say that there were interesting unclimbed 7,000-metre peaks in the Saser Kangri massif. One was called Plateau Peak and had been approached in the past from the Sakang glacier. The other was a peak of 7,017 metres with no name on some maps and simply absent from others. On yet another map it was called Chamshen, though Divyesh Muni wondered if the name was just a convenient invention in the absence of local knowledge.

Who could resist an offer like this? Unclimbed 7,000-metre peaks are an endangered species. I picked up the phone at once and called my artist friend Andy Parkin.

'Andy, you have to meet me at the pub … Yes, tonight … Because we have plans!'

Thirty years earlier the Alpine Club had received a similar invitation from the Himalayan Club, although then it was a letter through the post and Mumbai was still Bombay. Harish Kapadia was proposing to lead an Indo–British expedition to the Rimo massif just a few kilometres from the Saser group Divyesh was planning to visit. I was lucky enough to be part of that expedition. During that trip, we had the dubious benefit of being woken every morning at 7 a.m. sharp by shellfire. It was the military morning chorus, announcing that the struggle for control of the Siachen glacier had begun for the day.

The odd thing is I was connected to this war, in a rather roundabout way. In 1980 I had my first trip to the Karakoram, indeed, to any large mountain group. The attraction of the region was its sheer size and remoteness, and the hostility of its environment. The Karakoram hosts the world's largest glacial systems outside the polar regions: something that did not escape the notice of the great photographer Galen Rowell.

In early 1980 Rowell and his teammates Ned Gillette, Dan Asay and Kim Schmitz completed the ski tour to end all ski tours. With telemark skis and fifty-kilogram backpacks they started from the Pakistani village of Khaplu near Skardu on 27 March. Some 460 kilometres later they had skied up the Bilafond glacier, down the Lolofond, up the Siachen, down the Abruzzi, Gasherbrum and Baltoro glaciers, up the Biafo, passing under Conway's Ogre, across Snow Lake, and down the Hispar glacier, arriving in the Hunza valley on 8 May 1980. This ski traverse of the Karakoram was a magnificent conception and achievement, recognised by its prominence in the pages of the *American Alpine Journal*.

Reading through the article now, it is easy to see that Rowell and Gillette somewhat glossed over the issuing of permits and border crossings. One would guess they left this issue ambiguous on purpose without realising that this ambiguity would precipitate one of the longest-lasting wars of modern times.

While they were touring, Will Tapsfield, Cairns Dickson and I were packing to climb Conway's Ogre, overlooking the Biafo and part of their route. We arrived two months after they left. The Conway's Ogre expedition left the three of us so exhausted that it was another four years before I regained the energy to return to the Karakoram. I don't think that Will and Cairns ever did go back.

During the trip, we had been involved in the rescue of Koji Okano, a member of the Japanese Latok IV expedition. Okano sent us, by way of appreciation, a copy of *Mountains of the World* in Japanese, which showed that in the Hunza valley there was a huge unclimbed mountain just five kilometres from the nearest road with a valley base just a short walk from the nearest village. The mountain was called Bojohagur Duanasir. The opportunity was almost too good to be true, and definitely too good to wait for the competition to notice.

Four years after Conway's Ogre, I found myself teamed up with Phil Butler on this Bojohagur. Then we met the Japanese team climbing the same mountain from the 'other side'. It was this group that would claim the first ascent. Their presence was something of a surprise for us; we were pretty sure we were the only folk scheduled to climb this particular peak. We discovered the Japanese team had read Rowell's report and had planned to use the same route as the Americans to access the Siachen. They had been given permission by the government in Pakistan to climb the Rimo peaks on the left bank of the Siachen glacier.

Unfortunately for the Japanese team, the Indian army had also read Rowell's report and moved to occupy the passes overlooking the Siachen glacier. The Japanese team were blocked from reaching Rimo. The Pakistani army reacted, and so the Siachen war began, precipitated by, though not caused by, an article in the *American Alpine Journal*.

The following year, in order to prove that occupation is ownership, the Indian government gave Harish Kapadia its permission for an Indo–British team to climb in the Rimo massif. As a part of that expedition, I made an attempt to climb Rimo I with my friend Stephen Venables. It was Harish who told Divyesh to contact me. So now, thirty years later, here we were again.

Our local bar, the Micro Brasserie de Chamonix, or 'MBC', was crowded as usual on a Friday night. I was sipping the house-brewed Granite IPA, as close as you can get to British beer here in the Chamonix valley. No one noticed as the swing doors parted and a rather dishevelled artist limped into the room: Andy Parkin.

In 1984, the year I was on Bojohagur, Andy had suffered a major accident guiding near Zermatt, falling twenty-five metres and breaking everything on his left side. His doctors initially said he wouldn't walk again. He has no spleen, his left elbow is fused at right angles and his left hip is fused to the femur. When he did learn to walk again, the doctors said he wouldn't climb again. That challenge was also irresistible. He went on not only to climb but to do so at the highest level, creating hard new routes in winter in the Mont Blanc range, routes that have remained modern test-pieces thirty years later. All with his left side immobilised.

I was in awe of Andy when I migrated to Chamonix at the turn of the millennium, but not so in awe as to avoid him totally. We climbed occasionally in the Alps and a couple of times in Nepal. We'd spent December 2002 in Langtang, triple-carrying up the Langtang glacier, running out of food, starving and cold. Andy demonstrated his talent for survival, while I showed him I hadn't learnt from my experiences with Rafael on Nanga Parbat.

Andy flashed his enormous smile.

'Ah, hello Victor … ' And then he was greeting his other friends. 'Greenie, how are you? Nadesh, *tu vas*?' And so on.

'Pint, Andy?'

'Go on, then. Don't mind if I do.'

'Andy, I was just wondering … '

I hesitated a moment for his suspicious glance to pass. He was right to be suspicious. I was about to ask him to join me in an enterprise to a mountain whose name we did not know, of uncertain approach, bordering a war zone and with a Mumbai team we had not yet met.

'You are the very person I am looking for ... ' I continued.

And that is how it began. In the next few weeks, we acquired a third British member, Susan Jensen, a climber with Alaskan roots and a long list of serious Scottish climbs to her credit, working as a senior data analyst for the Scottish National Health Trust.

I can only assume that during the six months between January and July 2013, the Indian Mountaineering Federation (IMF) had an event horizon around it. Information flowed in, but not out. According to Hawking's radiation theory, pairs of particles pop into existence at the edge of a black hole's event horizon (for no good reason that I can fathom, but then I'm not a physicist), and while one twin is drawn inside the black hole, the other does manage to escape it. And that is where the analogy between a black hole and Indian bureaucracy fails, because while I know there are many pairs of random forms gene-rated by the IMF, I never actually saw one of them. This demonstrates rather neatly the law that information does not escape a bureaucracy but, like a singularity with no Hawking radiation, simply grows and grows. The upshot was that for months, we waited for the increasingly bloated Indian ministries to emit information about our permit, but to no avail.

'Do we or do we not have permission to climb yet?' Andy asked me every time we met. By 12 July, just a week before we were due to fly to Delhi, I decided I really ought to go to London to try and unblock the system.

In London, I was placed in the visa queue for two days only to discover the embassy could not process our passports because the IMF in Delhi had not sent our application forms to the London embassy. It looked like our expedition was sunk before it started. There then followed some extraordinary string-pulling on the part of Divyesh and Vineeta Muni. They had a relative who was a brigadier, who knew a general, who called the London embassy and spoke to an admiral, who agreed to push the visa department to accelerate our permits. I hadn't thought Andy and I would ever leave Europe, and yet two days later the whole British contingent was at the IMF briefing meeting in Delhi. Towards the end of the meeting, the IMF director, Colonel J.P. Bhagatjee, said:

'And, of course, you understand that satellite phones are expressly forbidden.'

'Please can you tell me why?' Susan always asked the direct question.

'You have been informed about the terrorist attacks in Mumbai? These people utilise satellite phones. That is why we restrict them.'

'But, what if we need … ' Andy stopped suddenly in mid-sentence as though Susan had kicked him under the table. We were not to know, but that ban would become rather significant.

Andy, Susan and I flew to Leh to meet the Indian contingent of our team as Divyesh and Vineeta arrived from Mumbai. In Leh we had briefings with the army and local police, and once more were reminded of the satellite phone interdiction.

The general plan was that the combined team would share the same base camp on the Sakang glacier. Then the British trio would explore the region in alpine style while the Indian pair would tackle their mountains in a more traditional style with Sherpa support.

Divyesh and Vineeta had sent food and expedition supplies over-land from Mumbai that seemed to have gone missing in their long trajectory from Maharashtra through Gujerat, Rajasthan, Punjab, Himachal Pradesh and Kashmir. This was a journey of over 1,500 miles, and on Indian roads had taken the best part of a month. When we arrived in Leh, the Mumbai supply truck was already three days late. In the absence of news, Divyesh had just convinced himself the bag-gage had been hijacked when it rolled into town in a cloud of dust. From the back of the truck leapt six dust-covered and bedraggled men: Divyesh's team of Sherpas and our expedition cook, whose name was either Chat-Up or Shut-Up. I couldn't quite hear the correct vowels.

From Leh, it was a ten-hour drive over a pass of 5,200 metres, the aptly named Wari La, to our road head; and then a four-day trek up to the snout of the Sakang glacier, looking for signs of previous camps. We reached our base on 25 July.

The first mountain we had intended to attempt was Plateau Peak, but on arrival at base camp we found the Indo–Tibetan Border Police Force camped nearby. They already had a team installing fixed ropes on the mountain. This was a mild surprise to us, although it shouldn't have been. The Indian army feels no need to inform the IMF of their expedition plans; we should have been expecting the unexpected.

The other team objective was the 7,000-metre peak with no name on some maps and non-existent on others. Divyesh had taken to calling it Chamshen. Unfortunately Chamshen was hidden behind Saser Kangri III. To reach it we would have to cross a pass, called the Sakang La, of 6,200 metres and descend the North Shukpa Kunchang glacier. The col had been reached three times before and the previous teams had all declared it uncrossable, although Google Earth suggested the crossing was quite feasible.

In hindsight, we should have had less faith in Mr Google. Though easy on the near side, the col turned out to be fairly lethal on the far side, the side descending down to the North Shukpa Kunchang glacier. The problem was that the far side faced east. It received the early morning sun, and though there was a snow-ice ramp leading down from the col to the glacier, every morning it was strafed by falling rocks as soon as the sun rose. We would have to cross before dawn.

Andy and I reached the top of the col for the first time on 1 August. It took us four tries to find a route that would be acceptable for the Indian Sherpas to follow safely. The col was in fact a serious climb in its own right.

'There's our route down the glacier,' I said, when we first reached the col. 'Looks a long way down here. If we can get down this side, we should be able to make it past that crevasse field.'

'Looks dangerous to me,' Andy replied pointing at the menace on the right side of the valley. 'If those séracs at the top of Saser II go, they could cover half the glacier.'

'I agree,' I said. 'But I think the main danger will be if the face accumulates enough snow in bad weather for the séracs to trigger a snow avalanche.'

I was thinking of events on Manaslu a year earlier, when a sérac triggered a catastrophic avalanche that killed eleven people inside their tents and sleeping bags.

'If the weather is good and the slopes aren't loaded, the debris shouldn't trouble us,' I added. 'But you're right, it is going to be a bit dangerous in bad weather.'

Looking down, we could see the glacier was more than a kilometre wide. If we could edge down the left bank, we should be reasonably safe from the séracs. Susan arrived at the col and we explained our thinking.

'There is a safe line down there in the middle. Looks like the left side is menaced by rockfall from Saser III to begin with and then the best line is down by the crevasse field on the left.'

'Why?'

'On the right, you see those séracs on the right?'

'So you're saying there is stonefall below us, more rockfall from the left, and avalanche from the right … looks like the Valley of Death,' she said. The name stuck.

On 10 August the entire Indo–British team crossed the Sakang La to the North Shukpa Kunchang glacier, into the Valley of Death. At 6,200 metres, the Sakang La would present a potential barrier to retreat. Just descending from the col was serious. The thought of re-climbing it on the way back, perhaps exhausted or in difficulty, was worrying. But what was even more menacing was the right side of the valley. This was the north face of Saser Kangri II. It was a 2,000-metre snow and ice face criss-crossed by enormous séracs, as Andy had pointed out from the col. We camped on the glacier, just far away enough from the sides of the valley to be out of stones' reach from Saser III and sérac fall from Saser II.

Next day, both the Indian and British contingents trekked down the Valley of Death and established a camp under Chamshen. After two days of exploration in indifferent weather, the Indians were planning to set up high camps and some fixed rope on the west side of Chamshen, while the British team had identified an interesting line on Chamshen's east face. Before trying that line, we needed to wait for better weather, and that meant we needed to get back to base for more supplies. The Sherpas had carried fifteen days' food and gas. It was all we Brits could do to bring five days' for the exploration. So on 14 August we set off for a resupply trip to base camp.

That was when the weather changed and it began snowing heavily. We were climbing back up the Valley of Death acutely aware that on our left, hidden in mist and clouds, were the now loaded avalanche slopes of Saser Kangri II. We had been caught in precisely the situation we wished to avoid.

After seven hours of effort, we were breaking trail through knee-deep snow and punching through numerous snow bridges into hidden crevasses.

'This is awful. We're going to have to camp soon; let's look at those ledges up there.' Andy was pointing at a feature to our right.

'But that's under Saser III. I can't remember what's above us. I don't think there's rockfall danger there, but I'm not sure.'

'Be safer than here.'

'Agreed. Problem is there are big slots to cross to get there, and at this rate it's going to take ages. What about moving on as far as possible to get close to the Sakang La – just another couple of hours?' I offered.

'Not the way I would do it.' But then Andy was always saying things like that. I was used to it.

'Two hours ... I'll break trail,' Susan said firmly.

So we continued, plodding on in the snowstorm. Through clearings in the cloud, we could glimpse bits of mountainside. By nightfall, we had erected our tents at the site of our first camp below the Sakang La, close to the left bank of the glacier between two large crevasses. We were at least a kilometre away from the loaded slopes of Saser Kangri II, and we judged this to be far enough to be safe from the séracs. We were partially right.

That night, Andy slept in a small one-person tent. Susan and I were in the slightly larger two-person tent. The porches were angled towards each other so we could easily share brews. Our ice axes had been co-opted for use as tent anchors. Outer boots in the porch. Inner boots inside.

At 10 p.m. we heard something from the direction of Saser Kangri II, something like a low rumbling, something sub-aural, felt more than heard. It was menacing.

Andy said, 'Better zip up! Like, it's a proper big one coming. And y'know what's gonna happen.' He was expecting a significant dusting of snow. Susan zipped up our tent. There was complete silence for about a minute, an eerie silence.

'I wonder if—' I began to say. And then the windblast arrived.

It hit us like a train. Something went over our heads. It was Andy in his tent. Our tent turned over and began to roll along the glacier. I felt no fear, just a realisation that I was not in control of my destiny. I don't know how far we rolled: at least thirty metres, and maybe fifty. As the tent rolled, we rolled inside it. It was like being inside a washing machine with another person.

I was fully aware this could be the day that I died. There were crevasses either side of the tent. Would the windblast blow our tent along the snow between the slots or into them? My one semi-rational thought was, 'Where is it? Where is the nearest crevasse?'

Then the wind eased and the tent came to a rest. It felt like half the tent was over a hole. It wasn't, but it took a few minutes of careful shuffling round in the dark to discover we were still firmly on the surface.

In fact, our tent had come to rest two metres from a bottomless crevasse and it had collapsed around us. Susan sat up, shaking off powdery snow that had been blown through the zip. We were still wearing our head torches and could see that the tent poles were bent but not broken.

'Your glasses are on your face,' Susan said before I could ask.

It took a while to sort ourselves and count what we still had. I was missing both my outer boots and one of the inner boots. The food and stoves were gone. The ice axes had disappeared. Most of the climbing equipment had disappeared. But I had the rope. Susan and I still had our climbing harnesses. The GPS and radio were missing, so we could not call Divyesh to let him know we were in trouble. Our illegal satellite phone, however, was still in the tent.

It was forty minutes before we were sufficiently organised to get out of the tent. With my neoprene overboots on over my socks, I waded around in the snow in the dark looking for missing items and shouting for Andy.

Wisps of snow scurried across the weak beam of light from my headlamp. The glacier surface had been scoured by the windblast, like a plane shaving wood.

It became clearer to me what had just happened. There had indeed been a catastrophic avalanche from Saser Kangri II. The snow itself hadn't reached us, but in falling two kilometres down the mountain's north face, the avalanche had generated winds strong enough to catapult Andy's tent over ours and send us across the glacier like floored bowling pins. If the avalanche snow itself had flowed across the glacier to reach us, there would have been no survivors. We would have been buried in our tents.

'Andy!' I shouted. 'Andy!' No answer. While looking for Andy, I found both my outer boots near our tent. My heart was pounding as I ran between crevasses shouting and hoping. It was a bleak feeling in the dark. What I was doing seemed hopeless and pointless. After so many years, I feared I had finally lost a climbing companion, a friend. All those Himalayan climbs had finally caught up with me. I was bursting with anxious frustration.

'Nothing. I can't find any sign of him.'

'I think I can hear a whistle,' Susan replied.

I could only hear the wind and my pounding heart, but there was a luminescence, a ray of light shining out of a crevasse hole where Susan was pointing. I put on my harness, tied on the rope and went to investigate.

The windblast that had thrown Andy over our tent had deposited him on top of a crevasse. As Andy ripped through the bottom of his tent, still inside his sleeping bag, he was plunged down into the narrowing jaws of the slot beneath. Rattling down the crevasse head-first, Andy had ricocheted between its walls, being battered in the process, until a snow bridge stopped him, about fifteen metres down. Just to be clear, that is the equivalent of falling off the roof of a five-storey building. In the dark. Imprisoned inside a sleeping bag. Upside down. He was then caught in a shower of his possessions and bits of broken tent. When that dried up, he took stock of his situation.

Andy's fused left arm had become stuck in the width of the crevasse, holding him upside down. His gloves were missing and so he began scraping away at the ice under his elbow with the fingernails of his free hand. After about an hour's scratching, he managed to free his elbow and flip the right way up.

Still in his sleeping bag, which was now wet and heavy, Andy spotted a source of light in the snow at his feet. It was his head torch. Having recovered it, he could now see how far he had fallen. He could also see that the snow bridge wasn't that big and that the crevasse continued deep into the glacier. Had he fallen to either side of the snow bridge, he would be dead. Andy was also pretty sure that the blast had been so violent that he was now the sole survivor of our group. He began looking for ways he might be able to climb out. It was when he pointed the torch up to look at the lip of the crevasse that we on the surface had our first clue that Andy had survived.

Before going down the crevasse to look for him, I had to make sure there was a proper anchor for the rappel. If the anchors failed, there would be no happy homecoming for me. I needed an anchor that could take the weight of both Andy and myself, while at the same time tying down our one remaining tent. As long as the weather was bad, there were sure to be more avalanches. If there was another blast while I was down the hole, we might lose the tent for good.

The surface of the glacier consisted of deep unconsolidated snow: useless for belays. The solution was found in the neighbouring crevasse; lowering carefully over the edge, I was able to go deep enough to find solid ice for our screws. This ice-screw anchor gave me the confidence I needed to rappel down to Andy. I tied the tent to the ice screws with the climbing rope and then lowered myself slowly over the edge, showering Andy with ice debris as I rappelled down to him.

He seemed unusually pleased to see me.

'Victor, I thought you were dead,' he said, shaking off the ice particles I had sent down.

'I thought the same.' I wanted to make a flippant riposte, but that didn't seem quite the time and place. My brain was not in the mood; it had switched into what chess players call 'only move' mode. I understood exactly what I had to do next, that there was no choice, and that it had to be done without error.

Before giving my friend the biggest possible hug for being alive, I clipped him into the rope. You never know when a snow bridge is going to collapse. I could not help noticing that this one was just three metres wide. If Andy had fallen into any other part of that crevasse, he would likely have been too deep to retrieve even if he had somehow survived the fall.

That was just one more break that had gone our way. There had been quite a lot of them. We had all slept with our harnesses on, which we might not have done. I had kept the crevasse rescue kit inside my sleeping bag, while all our other climbing equipment had been blown away. The satellite phone survived, but our other communication and navigation instruments had been lost. All food and stoves were gone, but we still had clothes, gloves and hats. We had two pairs of crampons and two ice axes between the three of us, enough to descend the glacier but not climb over the Sakang La. When he broke through the floor of his tent, Andy's boots fell with him and landed on the same snow bridge. My boots were found near my tent. And finally, Andy usually slept with the rope for a pillow, but I had been sitting on it to cook the night before, and had forgotten to pass it across to his tent. It was as if the local gods had been playing games with us, leaving us with just enough to stay alive, but no more.

Andy's sleeping bag was now soaked through. Although it was below freezing on the surface, there was water dripping inside the crevasse.

'I can't feel my feet,' he said.

Worried, I slid my hand gently down his spine feeling for lumps or bleeding.

'Can you tell me what you feel now?'

'Back is okay, just my feet are numb.'

Andy's feet were wet and icy cold. I removed his socks and massaged them till the feeling came back and then I pushed and squeezed them into his wet boots.

A shower of snowflakes floated down.

'Seems like another avalanche passing over,' Andy said.

'Susan is on top, watching the anchor and making sure the tent doesn't blow away again.' Above ground, Susan was in the tent being battered by this latest blast. I was a little concerned about being buried in the crevasse should the avalanche snow flow this far. We needed to get out.

Using crevasse rescue techniques, it took another two hours to haul Andy out. He was paraplegic with cold and bruising from his fall. He could not even crawl. We dragged him inside the tent, where Susan looked after him while I rappelled down the crevasse again to retrieve his rucksack and whatever else I could rescue from the snow bridge. Back on the surface, I tidied up as much as I could, coiling the rope and bringing inside anything I could see within the narrow beam of my headlamp.

It was 2 a.m. before I could join the others. We had just a litre of water between us and no stove or food. It was still snowing, big flakes blowing round the tent. More avalanches would come. All we could do was shiver together with cold as we waited for the next big blast.

At 5 a.m. the next blast arrived. The tent billowed like a sail and bent around us, but this time, with the weight of three bodies and the ice screw anchors, it remained in place.

We sat there just looking at each other. There was no need to voice our thoughts. We all knew we had to escape this place as soon as possible. Andy's crampons had gone, and in any case he was too damaged to climb. We would not be able to get up the Sakang La. The only alternative was to look for Divyesh and hope they hadn't left Chamshen base before we could reach it.

We left at first light. I gave Andy all the dexamethasone and pain-killers we had and, dividing the contents of his rucksack with Susan, we started down the glacier. Andy made heroic efforts to walk under his own steam, but it was awfully slow, stumbling and slipping into every crevasse we stepped across, or else collapsing with exhaustion at ten-minute intervals.

It took us until mid-afternoon to emerge from underneath the dangerous north wall of Saser Kangri II. Now safe, we could pitch the tent at the junction of the west and north branches of the North Shukpa Kunchang glacier. Then, having made Andy as comfortable as possible, we left him with the remains of our water and went to get help.

Slowly, painfully, Susan and I broke trail up the north branch of the glacier to Chamshen base camp, which we reached at nightfall. Divyesh and Vineeta took us in; for now, at least, our ordeal was over. We were with friends.

'How many gods have you got in India?' I asked Divyesh.

'Hindu gods? Approximately 6,000. Why?'

'They've been playing games with us. They left us just enough pieces to complete the puzzle. They took away all our equipment except the barest essentials.'

All we had to do now was extricate Andy.

In the morning we used our illegal satellite phone to call friends of Divyesh in Mumbai. They called a cousin who knew a general who called the local air-force commander who told us a rescue helicopter would be organised. Meanwhile, I walked back down the glacier with Divyesh and the Sherpas. The Sherpas were rested and much fitter and stronger than me, so they got to Andy long before Divyesh and I did.

When I reached the tent, the Sherpas were standing round it looking rather solemn. I was horrified. Had Andy died in the night?

'Divyesh, what are they doing outside the tent?'

'It is okay, Victor,' Divyesh replied. 'He is having a pee and they are showing respect.'

Sometimes, I thought to myself, I appear to be a paranoid idiot.

I made an improvised rope stretcher, a trick I had learnt in my nerdy youth, and the Sherpas demonstrated their strength and endurance carrying Andy back to Chamshen base camp, post-holing in the deep snow and passing him like a parcel across the collapsing surface of half-frozen streams.

Next day, the Indian air force (may all their gods bless them) arrived to evacuate Andy. The cloud ceiling that day was 5,800 metres and we were at 5,600 metres, meaning that the helicopters couldn't come over any high passes to reach us. Instead, they followed the steep-sided valley of the Shyok River for 200 kilometres before turning up the Shukpa Kunchang glacier. It was an amazing bit of flying. The two little space-framed Lamas wobbled off down the glacier just under the lid of the cloud.

After they had gone, I turned to Divyesh. 'Interesting they came with two choppers. I suppose if one has a problem the other can help.'

'Maybe,' replied Divyesh. 'But we are close to the border. Perhaps if one deserts, the other can shoot it down.'

'Really?'

'No. Of course not. Only joking.'

'Really?'

The helicopters had been able to fly up the Shyok River, but we couldn't have walked out that way; in mid-summer, the Shyok was in full flood, brimming over its banks and flooding the trails. We were going to have to go back up to the Valley of (Near) Death.

The air force flew Andy to the military hospital serving the Siachen area, and the following day to Leh hospital. As soon as they saw the X-rays, the staff wanted to send Andy to Delhi for emergency surgery.

'Wha … ? Why?'

'Your elbow, sir; it is badly broken!'

'That was thirty years ago. It's meant to be like that.'

'And then there's your hip, in need of reparation!'

'Naw, that's been that way for thirty years too.'

Andy became an unusual medical exhibit. The doctors said they had never seen such a broken-up body still moving around.

Meanwhile, I understood I was in for the legal high jump. The army now knew I had a satellite phone. Whatever the humanitarian purpose, it was expressly forbidden. As soon as we used the phone, the army would report us to the police. We might as well make the most of it.

So, using the phone again, we called for a weather update. We had three days of fine conditions ahead. Andy was safe, retreat to across the Sakang La uninviting. The best thing to do was to attempt the first ascent of Chamshen.

Susan and I had a rope, crampons and one axe each but, apart from our crevasse rescue kit, no other climbing gear. I was also still missing an inner boot. Since we also lacked food and a stove, Divyesh and Vineeta kindly gave us four days' supplies. We wandered up to the high camp below Chamshen, and the following day the entire team made the first ascent of the mountain, following the relatively easy west ridge. Although the top was at 7,017 metres, we were by now so well acclimatised that we could dance and sing on the summit. We didn't do that, but we could have done.

The day after the summit, Susan and I trekked up the Valley of Death during the night to reach the Sakang La before the sun did.

It was a complete contrast to our previous journey there. The stars were scattered across the clear black sky; the snow was crisp and firm to walk on. By the end of the day, and a very long day it was, we were back at Sakang base camp where Chat-up the expedition cook greeted us warmly and fed us generously. Our poor liaison officer had had no communications with us during the entire episode and had no idea anything had gone amiss.

It took three days, three long days, to walk down to the road head. I was getting extremely tired and hungry. The psychological effect of the avalanche was taking its toll. At the Tiggur Hotel, not far from the banks of the Nubra River, the waiter bowed as he brought us our curries.

'Please, sir, the police have come to arrest you.'

I stood up as quickly as my battered body would allow. The waiter pressed me back into my seat.

'It is okay, sir. Please finish dinner. They will wait for you upstairs.'

The food was delicious: lamb curried in tomatoes. There were fresh fruits and sweet sticky desserts.

After dinner, I went upstairs to be arrested. The officers were very polite. They wanted to confiscate the phone and asked for a lift to Leh in the morning. They didn't seem to have transport of their own. There was one more thing they needed.

'When you are in Leh, you must say you spent this night in Diskit jail. Not in Tiggur Hotel.' Diskit was an hour's drive away.

'Why?'

'It is better.' He gave me a look that said, 'Why the stupid question?'

Leh has strong links to Tibetan culture. Ladakhi is a dialect of Tibetan. So it was not too surprising when the district and sessions court judge turned out to be a middle-aged woman in Tibetan clothing. She spoke with an impeccable Home Counties accent. And in keeping with that accent, she spoke down at me as if I was some kind of idiotic juvenile criminal.

'So, Mr Saunders, you lied about the satellite phone.'

'But it was an emergency, your honour.' She cut me off sharply.

'That is of no consequence here,' and continued her theme. 'You saw the posters at the airport?'

'Yes.'

'You understand English, I take it?'

'Yes … but … '

'No "buts", Mr Saunders. You knowingly contravened our laws. That is a criminal act.'

I had not been treated like this since school. She was either a very fine actor or completely devoid of compassion. And then it got a bit more serious.

'We are going to charge you under the 1885 Telegraph Act. Violation of section 4/20 carries a mandatory sentence … '

'Yes?' I was all ears.

' … of seven years in jail.' She waited for me to digest this before continuing. 'But we won't charge you under 4/20. We will charge you under other sections, which incur a fine. Do you understand?'

'Yes,' I said quietly.

'You will write a confession and we shall deal with you now. Otherwise you will be sent to Delhi for trial.'

I could guess pleading not guilty was not the best option. Delhi courts have a very long waiting list. It could be years before my case came up. My only fear was that they might renege on the plea bargain. I need not have worried. The judge was as good as her word. My fine came to a little over $30.

'But 1885, isn't that British law?' I asked.

'Yes, it is.' She turned to her clerk and said a few words in Ladakhi to confirm I had paid my fine. Turning back to me, she continued. 'Thank you for paying your fine promptly. We will not enter the judgment on your passport. You are welcome to return to India. But, please, do not break the law again.'

And thus was I dismissed.

12

TREPPENWITZ

On Chamshen, we had understood danger would come from the séracs of Saser Kangri II, triggering massive snow avalanches in bad weather. We had assessed our position on the glacier as being safe from sérac fall. Though we underestimated the power and reach of the avalanche windblast, and as a consequence suffered a near disaster, we made reasonable decisions given what we could see at the time. By contrast, in the avalanche on Mont Maudit, when Roger Payne lost his life, I expected the weak layers to be on the right flank of the north face of the mountain. But I was wrong. The slopes that slid were on the left side. Starting late that day had been the correct decision. But I had made the right choice for the wrong reasons. We learn from our mistakes, or are meant to. Yet when we survive a poor decision, it can be hard to recognise it as such.

Years later I was still thinking about that. As mountain guides, we teach avalanche awareness courses. We teach decision-making, drawing on the information sources available. And yet, we frequently forget that we are essentially placing a bet on the outcome. We are always playing a percentages game.

It was February. I had just had a major physical setback – a retinal detachment – and the day after the emergency surgery was feeling very sorry for myself. I decided to drown my sorrows in paper and ink, and write a note to myself: 'Risk Management and Avalanches'.

But first, and I could not (can never) help this, there was a bit of displacement activity. I watched my favourite chess column on YouTube. Black was doing well. White had tried to set up a defensive fortress but had run out of safe moves. It was unfortunate, but any move White made would end in loss. It was *Zugzwang*, the forced move.

As a climber, I find there is much to learn from chess. There are the chess-like problems to solve, moving body parts like chess pieces. But also, some of the Yiddish chess expressions describe climbing situations so much more precisely than climbing jargon does. *Zugzwang* is a good example: can't move up, can't move down but you can't hang on forever. The position is not lethal ... until you're forced to move.

The thought brought back memories of an afternoon decades ago on Holyhead Mountain. My eyesight was better then, even though I have been myopic and have worn thick glasses since my schooldays. I had soloed into a slightly overhanging finger crack; the jams were in the wrong sequence, left-hand thumb up where it should have been right-hand thumb down. My feet were hidden from sight by a bulge at the level of my stomach. The ground had somehow withdrawn fifty feet lower than it had been a few seconds earlier and was now far too distant to invite a jump.

'What do you think?' I heard a concerned voice ask. There was something distinctly odd about the voice, but I was too preoccupied to boulder that one out. I answered as calmly as I could.

'As my friend Nick Kagan used to say, I think ... that we both think ... that we should not be here.'

It was *Zugzwang*. And I still shudder at the thought of that moment.

There is more from chess. That day I climbed like a beginner, a blunderer, a bungler: a patzer. And again, if you set up the board in public, often there is a bystander, the onlooker who offers unwanted advice. This is the *Kibitzer*.

'I will try to reverse the move and get my hands the right way round ... ' I said to myself.

'You can't climb down … you can't see your feet … you'll just have to pull and go up,' said the *Kibitzer* from far below.

'I can't pull … I can't reach … it's too far.'

'Pull hard, and then go off the edge of the crack on the way to the jug. A double movement. *Zwischenzug*. Just do it quickly.'

Zwischenzug: the in-between move. The unexpected move your opponent can't ignore. And so I pulled, knowing this was my only chance. I swiftly touched the edge of the crack, and the *Zwischenzug* allowed me to slide my fingers up again to reach and cling on to the bucket-sized thank-God life-saving jug that had previously been out of reach. Panting asthmatically, I flopped into the scratchy grass and thorns that occupy the clifftops at Gogarth. Looking back over the edge of the cliff, holding tightly on to branches of gorse, I could see no one at the base of the cliff. There was nobody there to thank. The *Kibitzer* was gone. I still don't know how that happened. I don't think he had time to become bored and walk off. Perhaps he was there in spirit only. I was in North Wales and there is sorcery in that ancient land. Or maybe he was never there at all. Perhaps the *Kibitzer* was in my head. If I could hear the voice again, I might recognise it in my mind's memory.

There was a loud knocking at the door. I closed the computer and let in Ben Tibbetts, accompanied by a flurry of snow. It had been snowing all night and all day, bringing the most dangerous avalanche conditions – Level 5 – to the Chamonix valley.

Two days earlier, Ben had been injured in a large avalanche that enveloped two of his party of three. They were on the second lap of a route they knew well. (He knows it even better now.) In Level 3 conditions, he had been looking out for the usual signs of windslab: that firm layer of snow the wind lays on a leeward slope on to a softer base. Triggered by a skier, windslab will slide like a magic carpet. Finding nothing conclusive, he stopped on a small shoulder to watch his two companions come down. They were all experts, and yet two of the three were about to be taken for the big ride.

Watching from the shoulder, he saw Lara trigger an avalanche and sink into the crumbling snowslab. The cracks propagated widely, and almost at once he realised that the avalanche included his part of the slope. Fear gripped him. There was no chance he would be able to ski away before the avalanche took him. Overpowered and helpless, he was carried down the slope and dumped, wrapped round a small stand of trees, buried upside down with one arm sticking out. His mouth and throat were packed with icy snow. You can't avoid inhaling snow-air while in the washing machine. (Don't believe people who insist you should shut your mouth. You still have to breathe, even if it is a snow-air mixture. Furthermore, as far as I know, there is no ethical way of testing the value of instructions to 'roll' or 'swim' once you are caught.)

Lara slid out of the bottom of the avalanche unharmed. Stuart, the third member of the party, reached Ben within a minute and dug the snow from Ben's mouth as he was passing out from lack of air. Had Stuart not done this so quickly, Ben would not have survived. He had dislocated his arm and torn ligaments in his knee, but these were trivial in comparison to his near-suffocation. The thought was horrible. Ben wouldn't be able to ski or climb until his shoulder and knee recovered, so here he was for lunch. After lunch, we drank coffee as Ben told me his avalanche story. A question came into my head, a curiosity, an itch I just couldn't resist scratching.

'Ben.'

'Yes?'

'You observed the conditions. You covered almost the same ground twice. You dug a few pits. You knew the slope and its avalanche history. As a guide, you are an expert. You teach avalanche awareness. What lessons are we learning from your escape? What is the enemy here?'

'The enemy? I guess it's the avalanche because it doesn't know you are an expert.'

'But how do we know we really are experts? I mean, if we are experts, why are we caught in avalanches?'

'Victor ... what are you saying?'

'I don't know, something I cannot put my finger on. We do avalanche-awareness courses, we teach the stuff. And yet ... '

'Eh?'

'I mean, if they don't stop us being avalanched ... ' There was something there; an idea hiding in his story. But I just couldn't get to it.

'Are you saying we should *not* do avalanche courses?'

'I'm not sure what I mean.' And I meant it. The itch was there; I just couldn't find the right place to scratch.

'I'm off to see the Nuptse guys' lecture tonight. Be good to see someone else doing stupid, dangerous things for once.'

'But how do we know? I mean, what ... ?'

'Bye,' Ben said firmly. I caught hints of boredom and frustration. He stepped out into the snowstorm. I climbed back up my steps, coffee in hand.

I felt defeated, irritated by my lack of clarity. It was like that after the retina operation. I couldn't see with my right eye. I bumped into things and my brain stumbled over the simplest ideas. It was all connected and it was maddening. And then, on the third step, my knotted thoughts began to unravel.

The steps. Of course, the steps! I had found the classic *Treppenwitz* response. You have family arguments. You give up in disgust. You stomp off upstairs, up the steps, *die Treppe*, and then, suddenly, you find the precise, defining riposte just as it's too late. This is *Treppenwitz*. (The French call it *l'esprit de l'escalier*.) Not a chess word, but really it should be, given the number of times I would like to have taken back my calamitous last move.

Of course! I understand now. Avalanche courses are good for describing avalanches; they just don't help us to predict them. We know they occur in slopes of a certain angle, and yet these are the very slopes we want to ski. And the proof that you can't predict those slopes is that experts are forever coming unstuck on them. QED.

I was lecturing an empty house.

There are some things we can predict. For example, in 2009 it was clear that the séracs on the West Shoulder of Everest would collapse at least once during the expedition season. It was possible to estimate the track of the flow, and how much of the trail from Everest Base Camp to Camp 1 the ice avalanche would take out. Inputting the time climbers would spend in that zone would give a percentage probability of being involved in the ice avalanche. The best assumptions gave the average climber a 0.83 per cent chance of being caught in the avalanche for that year. In reality, the actual number of people caught in the avalanche of 2009 was 0.75 per cent. On the other hand, there are things we quite simply cannot predict, when we don't have the information to input even the most basic assumptions to calculate. And ... avalanches are exactly that kind of thing. We can describe them, but the information needed to predict them is hidden from us.

> *So, thinking we are experts makes us our own worst ... no ... wait. Wait! Ben, it's like this ... Ben, we already know the enemy, we know it really well. Look in the mirror. The enemy is us!*

Only, Ben was not there to listen. I gave up on the coffee, poured the rest down the sink and pulled a beer from the fridge. I turned off my inner voice and enjoyed the silence, like a man who has finally stopped banging his head against a wall.

I wrote down a title on the blank paper, thought hard for a bit about things we can predict and things we cannot. Then I gave up. I put down the pencil and rested my head on the notepad. I thought about those nice Yiddish chess words. And then I fell asleep, and snored a little.

13

THE SERSANK REDEMPTION

(2016)

Since mangling me in the boxing ring, Mick Fowler had built successful twin careers in the tax office and the remote Himalaya while I, having given up architecture to become a mountain guide, had relocated to Chamonix and was working across the globe. We had barely spoken to each other in the intervening years. In fact, we had drifted apart. Then, in 2015, the French translator and alpinist Eric Vola had the idea of combining chapters from our books, a sort of literary version of a mash-up, but in French. The book did well, winning the main prize at the Passy book fair that year. Working on this volume, *Les Tribulations de Mick et Vic*, and probably aided by some of Eric's excellent Sauvignon Blanc, we agreed to try one more mountain together. We were much older now, of course. In 2016 Mick was sixty and I was sixty-six years old.

I had two doubts. Were we now really too old to do this sort of thing? And having drifted apart before, would we, once again, be friends by the end of the trip?

Mick had built an extensive intelligence network over the decades and a report back from Martin Moran of a 'tremendous north face of linked White Spiders' led us to Himachal Pradesh and the ever-so-slightly elusive Shiv Sankar, or Sersank, or else the unnamed mountain, depending on which expedition reports we read. Elusive because one

British and two Italian expeditions failed to make much impression on it, while a Japanese team were told by the authorities they could climb the mountain, but only if they could find it, because it did not exist. This team turned back at the base of the steep summit block because, according to their timorous porters, Sersank was sacred. Fortunately for us, the nearest villagers held no such beliefs.

Much had changed in the world since the 1980s. Then we phoned from telephone boxes. The World Wide Web had still to be invented. There was no such thing as Wi-Fi. Expeditions were booked by post and we arrived home before our letters from base camp. Climbers spent days in custom houses releasing freighted supplies, and most of us did not know about local agents.

Now, with an email or two, all is arranged without leaving home. Our excellent local agent and fixer, Kaushal Desai from Manali, had us collected in Delhi, briefed by the IMF and on the bus to Manali with our liaison officer Sanju and our base-camp cook Devraj, all within the space of a few hours. Two days later we were trekking up the Sural valley to our objective. This logistical slickness was of course due to Mick's predilection for organisation. And so the programme continued at base camp:

Day 1: *unpack and set up.*
Day 2: *set off for acclimatisation and reconnaissance.*
Day 3: *reach the Sersank La, where we will gaze in wonder at the 'north face of linked White Spiders'.*

This would be the first glimpse of our project. Would the north face be climbable or seriously out of condition? When we reached the Sersank La, on schedule, Mick began leaping up and down with excitement.

'Vic! It's all there! To be honest, I was a bit worried it wouldn't be.' And then he continued ticking off his usual checklist of project requirements. 'Looks like an obvious line; straight to the summit; visible from afar;

challenging; unclimbed; different descent.' Then he paused. 'And it is such a pleasure to have such an experienced old climbing partner.'

'Pretty rich,' I mumbled. 'Ageist comments from a sixty-year-old pensioner.'

We continued with the Fowler itinerary.

Day 4:   acclimatise on a minor summit in front of Sersank.
Day 5:   back to base for exactly two days of R&R.

Our reconnaissance had shown the projected route to be threatened by a line of séracs, whereas a longer but safer line from the toe of a buttress on the left side of the face looked good to both of us. It seemed our ideas of what was safe in the mountains were still in harmony. At base camp I wrote a route description, giving expressive names to each section: the 'Dreaded Ridge', the 'Ice Hose', the 'Banana Icefield', 'Fun with Cornices', and so on.

After precisely two days of planned rest, and armed with six days of food and gas, we went back up and across the Sersank La and on to the face. The acclimatisation must have worked a bit. What had taken two days before now took six hours, but with thirty-kilogram rucksacks it still left us worn out at the start of the climb. Not the best place to be worn out.

Mountains change shape as you approach them. They usually go through three stages of appearance. From far away, they always look easy. As you approach the base, they begin to look hard. And finally, when you are climbing, the hard bits sometimes feel easy again: sometimes, but not always.

This time, on the approach, the mountain reared above our heads, reminding me a lot of our first climbs together in 1979. It looked a bit like the Orion Face on Ben Nevis, only on steroids and grown gigantic.

From close up, the north face looked confusing. I had been hoping to see icy runnels and grooves and other climbable features, but because of the perspective it was impossible to see the sequence of icefields we wanted to link together. The 'White Spiders' were hidden. Instead, there seemed to be a dark and dangerous-looking series of cliffs stacked on top of each other.

'Fuck, it's morphed into steep buttress climbing,' I said.

'Luckily, I have you to slip up those steep little bits of rock for me,' Mick replied with irritating optimism. 'And never fear, it will be perfect "twang" ice all the way.'

'Twang' ice is ice that takes an axe blow without splintering into plates; 'twang' ice leaves your ice tools vibrating nicely, like tuning forks. I gave Mick my best 'I remain to be convinced' look.

There was no moon that first night. At 4 a.m. Mick made our first breakfast brew. The stars were sprinkled against a black sky. A cold katabatic wind drifted over the tent. Mick's contact lenses were frozen, so he defrosted them on the tip of his tongue. We ate porridge and drank tea in the same plastic cup. Shivering with cold and anticipation, we folded away the icy tent and sleeping bags while pausing to blow on our freezing hands and then stuffing our frozen possessions into rucksacks. Poo and pee break. Crampons and harness on. It took an hour and a half before we got going on the first pitch.

The climbing was tiring and difficult in a way that wouldn't show in the photographs, mainly up unconsolidated snow on rock. The underlying rock was a kind of shitty shale or schist for the first dozen pitches. Later it would become a more pleasant granite or gneiss, but we weren't to know that at the time. Cleaning snow away with my mittens revealed the odd corner or crack that might take thin knife-blade pitons, but the rock was so fragile it held pegs only loosely. Whenever I was forced to do a hard move, stepping up as gently as possible on the tips of my crampons, I couldn't stop my mind going back to those pegs popping out of Astral Highway all those years ago. Pitch after pitch, we balanced up slowly with aching calf muscles, hoping not to test the pegs. Reaching the end of each pitch brought relief to the muscles but not my anxious mind.

By pitch seven on the first day it was already 3 p.m. Many of the pitches had taken over an hour to lead. The anticipated *névé* never appeared. In my diary, I wrote of the final pitch of the day, 'a very hard powder-on-rock pitch, leading to the Dreadful Ridge. Mick found the only possible line, zigzagging through the outcrops, searching for, and not finding, little bits of "twang" ice.' He wrote:

> The buttress was steep with powdery snow stuck to all but the very steepest rock. What looked to be straightforward from a distance was terribly precarious and painfully slow, involving clearing perhaps fifteen centimetres of snow, hooking crampon points over rugosities in the rock and teetering upwards. It was not until early on our second day that the ground changed as we reached the knife edge crest of the buttress … The way forward now was to traverse the sharp crest towards the face. It wasn't the kind of ground that was conducive to abseiling, and if we should fail higher on the face it was clear that we would have to reverse these pitches followed by a climb back over the Sersank La. That would be horrendous. I very much hoped we were good enough to get up.

We found a small snow ledge to put the tent on. It was just wide enough for one and a half of us, so we had to sleep partially on top of each other. There was also a pointy rock above that made sitting up impossible. The first gas canister was now finished, having lasted three days, which showed just how little water we had drunk, a litre and half each per day.

The objective the next day was a streak of ice reminiscent of the Ice Hose on the north face of the Eiger. The weather continued to be perfect, giving no excuse for thoughts of retreat (or, as I prefer to call it, 'running away'). The climb had begun to feel very committing to me. Looking down, the glacier already seemed a very long way away. I wondered how many abseils it would take. But that was not the worst of that long night. The katabatic breeze had got up again and there was a cascade of spindrift over the tent. The loose snow was filling the gap between the tent and the mountain, threatening to push us off. Using our plastic cups, we were trying to bail out the snow around the tent when, quite suddenly, without warning, I had an extremely urgent need to relieve my bowels. There was no time to lose. But first I had to get out of my sleeping bag, get a jacket on for the spindrift and then … too late. I was in a state of anguish. How was I going to continue the climb with my pants now filled with poo?

'Fuck! I need a nappy!' I said. I was really quite upset. 'What the fuck am I going to do now?'

Mick was cuddled up in his warm sleeping bag.

'Cut your underpants off with the Opinel knife,' he said helpfully.

And then he pointed his camera and took photographs as I set to work slicing off the offending garment and cleaning myself with snow as best I could. If Grania had magically appeared in that moment, as she had at the student party all those years ago, I would have said, 'He is definitely NOT my friend.'

It was a long night, and Mick made a small brew to cheer me up.

My only thought was the hope I had cleaned myself up enough to bear the next several days. I could not get back to sleep and neither could Mick. Finally, he said:

'I've thought all the thoughts I can think … and still can't sleep.'

I have to admit, that did cheer me up a bit.

On Sersank, most things were highly reminiscent of our former climbs. We recognised each other's climbing style. Together, we endured the discomfort of tiny bivouac ledges and spindrift showers, the miserably small portions of food (not being strong enough to carry more) and chatted aimlessly to pass the cold nights away.

The one big change in thirty years was the conversation. Where before it was the usual boys' blather, food and girls, now it was pensioners' talk. It could have been overheard on any golf course. Arthritic limbs and rheumatic joints, what to do about the children, failing eyesight and other interesting topics filled our hours of rest.

In my diary, I noted how our bodies were falling apart with age and overuse.

1. *Mick has separated the cartilage from his ribs, the result of a short fall in the Peak District. He is still in pain.*
2. *Mick cut the nerves in his fourth finger in the winter, and can't feel to know if he's getting frostbite.*
3. *Mick has a cold sore on his lip that won't stop bleeding.*
4. *Mick has some kind of painful boil on his chest, under the rucksack strap.*
5. *I can't eat. Our dehydrated food is giving me diarrhoea every day.*
6. *My fingers have developed excruciating cracks that won't heal. I can't do up my bootlaces. Mick does that for me.*
7. *My asthma keeps reappearing whenever I think about the descent.*
8. *My cataracts are making it difficult for me to see at dawn and dusk.*
9. *We both think we have memory loss, but can't be sure.*

Bit by bit we linked the icefields, the White Spiders. But in spite of the steady progress the outcome was never quite certain. In steep face climbing, the best line is far from evident, and again it was modern technology that helped here. In 1987 on Spantik I had drawn a detailed route diagram to help us find the way.[6] Three decades later we could examine photographs on our digital cameras. But we couldn't quite work out from the reconnaissance what the finish would be like. The headwall loomed over our heads and our imaginations. Would that be the final sting in the tail?

Meanwhile, every difficult pitch we climbed made retreat less inviting and increased our commitment to traversing over the top of the mountain. The entry to the Banana Snowfield was steep, but the ice, as it had been on most of the steep sections, was positive and

---

6   Victor and Mick made the first ascent of Spantik's Golden Pillar, one of the most beautiful routes in the Karakoram, in 1987. There then followed a twenty-nine-year gap in their climbing partnership before they reunited for the ascent of Sersank.

'twangy'. But to escape the north face we really had to find the hidden exit line to the 'Fun with Cornices' section. I led one more tricky pitch to exit the Banana Snowfield, a couple of off-balance moves, and suddenly we were in a kind of hanging valley, a vague ridge between us and the enormous face below and, rearing up above our heads, the line of cornices, some of them threatening and large, all of them overhanging.

Above me was a weakness in this line of overhangs. The route to reach it seemed like straightforward snow, but turned out to be a pitch of hard ice. There was no twang, just brittle plates of ice breaking off and slithering down towards Mick. My crampons were now blunt and needed an extra hard kick to gain purchase and stay stuck in the ice. My axes bounced off instead of biting. I was exhausted from five days of physical effort pushing big rucksacks up the mountain, the lack of digestible food and energy, and the neurosis that always accompanies me on committing outings.

My last runners were far away, but it was just too much effort to place lots of screws in that steel-hard ice. Finally, with fading strength, I smashed two holes with the ice hammer and twisted in screws for a belay. I was just beneath the narrowest part of the fringe of cornices. Mick looked slightly less tired than me when he arrived. He hung his sack on the belay and aimed himself at a section of cornice that only overhung for a couple of body lengths. He soon pulled over the fringe. It had all gone so quickly! I will always remember the look of happy surprise on his face when he looked back from the other side of the overhang. That huge smile said, 'Yes … we will live a little longer after all!'

We were now in the sun for the first time in a week, at around 6,000 metres. Slowly, we trudged towards a foresummit. The sun went down. Time to sleep. Cutting a platform in the snow, we discovered the ice was just below the surface and the only ledges we could manage were wide enough for a single person. It would be another head-to-toe bivvy. The lack of food was beginning to affect me. I was cold, but strangely not hungry.

The next day brought a straightforward summit, a descent to a comfortable tent platform and another cold night, followed in the morning by a complex and steep descent through the South Sersank glacier, which proved excessively crevassed and bristling with séracs. Once we got away from the glacier, we could take off the rope. It was now much warmer and we could pile our duvet jackets and warm clothes on top of the climbing equipment in our rucksacks. Mine became so misshapen the only way I could carry it comfortably was bent double, like a peasant in a Hokusai print.

Devraj and Sanju met us half an hour before the camp. They brought tea and *puri*. Then these dear kind men carried the rucksacks for us. I couldn't wait to get out of my shitty clothes.

In base camp we wallowed in a pleasant recovery haze: we ate our first real cooked food for nine days, dozed in comfort on flat ground without being tied into the mountain, and generally enjoyed the warmth and oxygen of the lower altitude.

Mick spent the following day in his sleeping bag.

'What are you doing?' I asked.

'I am staring at the tent fabric with pure pleasure, thinking about the climb. I am in a bubble of happiness.'

He was ticking off the adventure-climbing boxes. New route? Tick. Significant length? Tick. Sufficiently challenging? Previously unclimbed summit? Descent by a different route? All ticks.

But I knew my friend. By tomorrow, he would be planning the next adventure.

Meanwhile, I was in my own bubble, happy to have discovered that in our dotage, an ancient friendship had been redeemed. I lay in the dining tent trying to force my old brain to remember exactly which book it was that quoted Colin Kirkus: ' ... going to the right place, at the right time, with the right people is all that really matters ... '

What we did was purely incidental.

EPILOGUE

It's a cliché, I know, but really: expect the unexpected.

Encouraged by our success on Sersank, Mick and I were about to set off for yet another trip in October 2017 when he was diagnosed with lower bowel cancer. The chemo and radiotherapy were pretty awful for Mick, but after six months it looked like he was in remission. We postponed the expedition to October 2018. A week before leaving, Mick had a relapse. We had no choice but to cancel the flights for the second year in a row. The risk of the cancer spreading was too great for us to wait another six weeks while we were climbing. He needed surgery at once.

Mick acquired a colostomy and was left with a stoma and an email from a *Daily Telegraph* journalist who wanted to update his obituary. 'It's quite an honour!' the journalist wrote. Mick updated the final draft of his new book *No Easy Way* to include the email. In the spring of 2019 we finally made it to Sikkim only to find that part of India had just had the snowiest winter in sixty years. After burrowing around in waist-deep snow for three weeks we called it a day. We should have paid more attention to the advice we got from Julie-Ann Clyma. When Mick asked her about conditions in Sikkim, she replied, 'Just how much uncertainty can you take?'

I went off to make a ski ascent of Mount Logan with Dr Rick, followed by a summer guiding in Pakistan and the Alps before a second visit to Sikkim in October 2019. Once more, we were confronted by uncertain flights, intractable bureaucracy, monsoon-destroyed roads and closure of the mountains by the military. Once more, Mick showed his enormous persistence negotiating Indian red tape while our magical local agent displayed his prestidigitation skills in slipping our vehicle through forbidden zones. Once more, we found ourselves in the uninhabited valleys under Chombu. There was the seemingly obligatory two weeks of daily snowfall and wet snow plodding. We had arrived excited about the west face of the mountain, only to find rocks and avalanches pouring down the very gullies and couloirs we intended to follow. We ruled the west face out, and also other possible routes on the south end of the hill. That left the slightly shorter north face. Roger Payne and Julie-Ann Clyma had attempted this route in 2007, but found deep snow made it unclimbable.

By 13 October we had passed the crux of the climb – steep snow-covered buttresses – and broken out on to a (relatively) low-angled shoulder that led to the north summit of Chombu. It was day four. Most of the pitches for the previous two days had been physically demanding, spiced with the psychological uncertainty of uncon-solidated snow and sparse runners. Our sense of insecurity was not helped when I took a fall, my first in the Himalaya. The rope brought me to a stop after twenty metres. I was left dangling upside down near Mick.

'Slip? Why are you upside down? And why are you back here anyway?'

'Can you PLEASE shut up and keep the rope tight while I get myself the right way up.'

I was a little shaken by the length of the fall. Twenty metres is the equivalent of a six-storey building and I had not expected the runner to hold. 'And would you mind leading the next few pitches?'

By the time we reached the shoulder we were at 6,107 metres, barely 250 vertical metres of moderate climbing below the summit, though in the snow conditions we were experiencing we estimated that could take us another day and a half. That night, we shared a packet of dried food that was labelled 'Beef Stroganoff with Noodles'. It tasted strange, a bit like oxidised linseed oil, but we knew we needed the energy for the next day and ate it anyway. This was a mistake.

We started the night with five spare colostomy bags, one roll of toilet paper and a shared novel, Khaled Hosseini's *And the Mountains Echoed*. By dawn we only had two unused colostomy bags and had discovered the paper in your average novel was not as absorbent as we thought.

Mick was typically exact in his recall of this moment. 'As I tried to vomit next to the streaks of diarrhoea outside our little tent, the purity of the clear and crisp dawn was not lost on me, nor was the fact that the first rays of sun were catching the pristine summit 250 metres above us. Compared to what we had climbed thus far, the ground ahead looked straightforward.'

We had been so sick overnight there was no grown-up decision but to go down. We were not able to eat again for two days. We would have been risking hypothermia and frostbite had we pushed on. Half a year later I still wonder what would have happened if we had been thirty years younger. Mick and I don't speak about that. It is not his style. We made our decision and have to move on. And we have plans for 2021.

Mick wasn't my only friend to face uncertainty. In December 2015 Andy Parkin was with Simon Yates attempting an unclimbed peak on the Antarctic Peninsula when he pulled off a large rock. On its way down, it crushed the muscles on his right leg (the previously good one). It took two weeks of heavy weather sailing for Marcel the skipper to get him to the nearest medic in Ushuaia. The reaction among doctors there was the same as it had been in Leh two years earlier: they were concerned – and then amazed – by the extensive injuries from the accident in 1984. Once again he was a medical curiosity.

Andy had barely recovered from this latest insult to his long-suffering body when his studio in Les Praz burnt down. The following winter saw big snowfalls and the fire-weakened roof collapsed, rendering the space – *his* space – completely unusable. Three years later and the rebuilding project is finally underway. Meanwhile, Andy remains irrepressible. When he was a young man, he only had three topics of conversation: the arts, climbing and girls. Now we just argue about the arts and climbing. He is a near neighbour and we continue to dine together, sharing a bottle or two while arguing long into the night.

I didn't see so much of Rafael after our 1996 expedition to Nanga Parbat as I would have liked. A year after our trip, he and his BMW R90S hit an elk. The motorbike was a write-off and so, nearly, was Rafael. After a fortnight in a coma, he regained consciousness but remained in hospital for seven weeks. Rafael was left plagued by headaches and lack of sleep. It was, he said, 'a book in itself'. I didn't get much more detail; our phone conversations are generally plagued with terrible sound and lack of clarity, unlike our face-to-face conversations which have marginally better levels of sound. Rafael biked down to Chamonix to attend an international meet in 2001. Over the usual lubricants, he told me about his last expedition to Pakistan in 1999. With Ralph Høibakk and Torill Berg, Rafael said he was aiming to reconnoitre a new route on Tirich Mir to celebrate the fiftieth anniversary of the first ascent in 1950. On that expedition, the transport officer Tony Streather had reached the summit with his Norwegian teammates on his very first climb. Rafael's anniversary expedition did not take place; the route they were looking at was too dangerous. Rafael now divides his time between Denmark, where he indulges his passion for mountaineering history and gardening (I have plans to inspect the gardening work in Jutland), and Sweden, where he has been seen in his old climbing haunts around Gothenburg.

My mother, perhaps remarkably, perhaps not, is still with us at the time of writing, now in her early nineties. She never did take up climbing. I called Mum from New Zealand in June 2012 after climbing Everest with Jakob Lindquist. It had been a hard summit. Storms had forced us down from Camp 4 on our first attempt but we went back a week later. Climbing to 8,000 metres twice in a week is tough. At least this time I had remembered to carry the ashes of my father to the summit.

Hearing my report, Mum said, 'That's nice.'

'Not only that, I have now scattered his ashes on all the seven summits except Kilimanjaro.'

'Oh how lovely!' She was being polite. She had no idea what I was talking about.

'Yes, Mum. Got to make sure he can't recombine and come back to haunt us.'

While we'd been climbing Everest, Hugo had trekked up to base camp and was waiting for us to return, almost the best present a father can expect to have. Maggie, his mother, continues to live in Edinburgh; she says she will retire from teaching one day.

I called Maggie in 2016, returning to France from Sersank. 'Your son … ' she began.

Hugo was always my son when he had done something wrong.

'Your son has just gone and broken his ankle.'

'How did he do that?'

'The university's climbing wall.'

It was a surprise; I didn't know he had taken up the sport. Like both his parents, he would become obsessed with climbing. He now makes films and lives not far from Maggie in Edinburgh.

While in New Zealand, I was introduced to Arrowtown Bakery, famous for (probably) the best pies in the world. Then, in a remote valley near the small town of Cromwell, I knocked on the door of a large, rambling house. There were sheep roaming in the field behind the property. It took Nick Kagan a few minutes to register who it was standing there in front of him. It had been thirty-two years since we had last seen each other. In 1979 Nick had worn a beard and we both had shoulder-length hair. Now, what little hair we had left was tinged with grey. Or, more accurately, white.

Over beer and supper, he told me about how those years had passed. How he met Jude, his partner, about his two children and how he began his medical career in New Zealand in a rough mining town. In 1990 he developed non-Hodgkin's lymphoma. Among the symptoms Nick told me about was the feeling that his skin was covered in cobwebs. Orthodox therapies were not working, so he turned to alternative medicine, having, as he saw it, nothing to lose. He tried chanting the Japanese Buddhist mantra 'Nam Myōhō Renge Kyō'. It helped him. When Nick stopped the chanting, he felt worse again. Resuming the chanting brought not just relief but an apparent remission. As a reward, a present to himself, Nick trained as a mountain guide and qualified about the same time as I did. That led to a phase alternating helicopter ski work in India and medicine back home. After ten years, he had a relapse of the lymphoma, but once more the disease receded. I was intrigued and asked if he chanted through the second episode as well as the first.

'Kind of both, but I got introduced to chanting the first time, so it all went into the mix the second time. Now I kind of like doing it. I like the vibration sound it makes. It's kind of like how banging your head against a brick wall feels so good when you stop.'

I asked Nick how his fellow medics reacted to his miracle cure.

'Absolutely controversial. I was an outcast.' He thought for a minute and added, 'When you are running out of gas, chemo in my case … well, I kind of decided to try it out and see. My children said it made me a better person too. I've bumped into other staunch chanters who have had cancer and died from it, and some that have got better. I am not a full-blown believer, but if it works for you … '

Later Nick showed me his two hundred sheep; there was always something of the farmer about him. Then he showed me his pride and joy, his microlight.

A year later Nick crashed his microlight pretty badly, ending up in hospital and once again making a complete recovery. I did not get to hear about that until finishing off this book. Nick is now in semi-retirement, working as a weekend hospital doctor and, I suppose, a sheep farmer the rest of the time.

I only realised writing this that Nick has not lost his childhood catchphrase. 'I kind of … ', 'A-kana … ': 'Kana' Kagan, my old schoolfriend.

So, this is how my story ends: an old man remembering the past.

It is mid-April 2020. I have a strange sensation, that we, that I in particular, are enclosed in some kind of ephemeral dream where everything is normal. When I wake up, I find that we are in the middle of the first wave of the 2020 coronavirus crisis. The dream is a kind of reverse nightmare: a 'daymare'? A dream where instead of waking to find everything is all right after all, you wake to find reality is bloody awful; your friends and family are out of work, unable to pay their rent, afraid of the future and yet only the future can save them. I have no idea what the world will look like in a month from now, let alone a year when this little book will make its appearance.

By that time, kind reader, you will be seeing this episode from the other side of the daymare. You will know what happened across the world in this strange year. You will know things I do not know – yet. You will look on 2020 as if reading tales of another country, such is the past that I am writing to you from: tales from my already half-forgotten history.

ACKNOWLEDGEMENTS

In late November 2018 I landed at Calgary airport with a suitcase of jumbled notes and essays. I was headed for the Banff Centre for Arts and Creativity. In anticipation, I told everyone in my life that I would be unreachable for a month. I would be in retreat. Everyone at the Banff Centre was universally friendly and helpful; I was often seen wandering around slightly lost, looking for my room key or notebooks. I adopted a routine that was at once fruitful and moderately healthy: a short run and swim before breakfast set me up for each day's writing. I worked in the Evamy Studio, one of the Leighton Artists Studios. There I had space to spread out and organise my ideas. The cabin was set in a spruce and pine forest, and the local herd of elk often wandered past the windows. Days ended with a short session in the climbing gym. There were a few occasions when I met other artists. I saw a dress rehearsal of a contemporary dance company and listened in on a musicians' evening where artists showcased work they had produced at the centre. I was inspired by a novelist in a neighbouring cabin. These cross-disciplinary encounters were uplifting and the daily rhythm was a rhythm made in paradise. I looked forward to waking up every day and going to work. By the end of four weeks, I flew out with a first draft manuscript. None of this could have happened without the support of the Paul D. Fleck Fellowships in the Arts.

This little book owes a huge debt of gratitude and thanks to both the fellowship and the centre.

The fellowship was the result of a human chain reaction leading to the Centre. I have to thank all who were part of that accidental reaction. There are the climbers, of course, who have enriched my life. I also have to thank Eric Vola, who inadvertently got me writing again. Louis Marino and Karin Stubenvoll, friends from the Chamonix valley who emigrated to Canmore, were the sparks that triggered the whole thing. Their friend and mine, Jo Croston, instigated the fellowship. Hugo Saunders' artistic advice and inspiration more than once kept me working when I felt lost for words. I am grateful to Jon Barton of Vertebrate for believing these words worth publishing; to the staff at Vertebrate, especially John Coefield for his photographic advice and and Emma Lockley for her careful culling of my numerous mistakes; and to this book's editor, Ed Douglas, whose literary skills are only matched by his encouragement over the decades we have been friends. It was Ed with his cheeky start-up magazine *On the Edge* in the heady days of the 1980s, those days when we believed we could do anything, who persuaded me to start putting words on paper in the first place.

Victor Saunders
Les Houches
August 2020